i didn't want to either

i didn't
want to
either

TRANSFORMING THERAPY
from **DAUNTING** to **DOABLE**

Cody Qureshi

 **Ripples Media**

Published by Ripples Media
Atlanta, Georgia
www.ripples.media

For more information: contact@ripples.media

First printing 2026

Book and cover deisgn by Burtch Hunter

ISBN (Paperback) 979-8-9940073-1-0
ISBN (Hardcover) 979-8-9940073-2-7
ISBN (eBook) 979-8-9940073-0-3

For you—the reader who dares to hope
that life can feel different,
and who possesses the quiet bravery
to turn hope into action.

Contents

Foreword

by Margaret Ann Jessop, PsyD

Psychologist and author of the children's book series *Hornets & Hippos: How to Use Imagination, Mindfulness, and Brain Science to Decrease Fear and Anger and Reach Your Goals*

Rarely do you hear about a therapist's journey traveling their own road to find the right therapist. While many counselors and psychologists have stories about their own failures, insecurities, and areas of improvement, clients do not have the opportunity to see that therapists go through so many of the same struggles they do. *I Didn't Want to Either* is the unique opportunity for readers to learn about the process through the lens of another therapist. Through that process, Cody Qureshi provides a valuable guide to those who are interested in pursuing therapy, even if they don't know quite where to begin.

With grace and her own vulnerability, Cody shares that even licensed therapists need help getting started. It is with this authenticity that she shares knowledge about the road to therapy and the steps involved in treatment. Even for readers who may not be ready to start one-on-one therapy, she shares actionable insights and practices for readers to improve their mental health—simply by applying the tools outlined in this book. This book has incredible value to all readers, regardless of where you are in your mental health journey.

One of the hardest parts of finding support in our most troubling and anxious moments is that it is hard to think straight and take action confidently. As I like to say, "anxiety does terrible things to very nice people," and our world is full of situations that leave us uncertain and prone to second-guessing. Informed by her own clinical work with vulnerable immigrant populations, Cody has developed sensitivity that has helped her give clear guidance on how to approach therapy, and most importantly provides multiple tools to help, even if you're not ready to reach out to somebody else.

As a psychologist and educator, I have spent the majority of my career working in prevention programs for young children with anxiety and currently with adolescence in suicide prevention. I speak for a number of therapists in saying that we all wish we could minimize the need for what we do, tackling the upstream challenges instead of developing programs to treat a cascade of downstream effects later. We are honored to sit and listen to the stories of others to provide support. However, there is a critical need to assess issues earlier and provide upstream solutions. That is exactly what Cody has done in this book.

In any facet of life, it is always helpful to have a thoughtful friend who encourages us and reminds us, "You are brave and you can do this." Time and time again, Cody reminds readers of that in this book. Change is the only constant thing in our world and we can all start making our own changes today. Cody provides the healthy encouragement we all need.

Introduction

Anticipation tingles throughout my mind as I stare at my digital reflection, waiting for the first session to begin. How is this going to go? Perhaps they'll dive head-first into the problem, or maybe we'll slowly wade into the waters? I mentally tally the therapeutic resources I have at the ready—like Pokéballs waiting to be thrown into the action. The countdown continues as I look at my clock, and suddenly a little blue pop-up appears on my computer screen. I click "Admit" and put on my game face to meet my new client in our digital therapy space.

I greet my client with a warm smile and metaphorical passport in hand, ready to enter my client's world and travel with them on their mental health journey. New clients often come to me with nerves and trepidation. Because of the population I work with, I'm often the first therapist that they have ever met, and they're unsure of how the session will go. To ease them in, I respond with a carefully-crafted first session routine: weaving in humor, empathy, and professional curiosity to disarm the anxiety and set the stage for what our working relationship may look like. As the minutes tick by and we talk together, a merging forms as the client and I begin to get on the same wavelength and build a therapeutic alliance.

To be honest, as a therapist, I'm more than comfortable with first therapy sessions, no matter how nervous anyone is. In fact, I'm usually energized by them! I often find myself eager to meet the new client who will be taking the hot seat. But it wasn't necessarily this way for me as a client myself. Which is why my heart holds such deep respect and admiration for individuals who have recognized the need for help in boosting their mental health. The amount of courage it takes to bridge the gap between acknowledging the need for guidance, and actually getting set up for that very first therapy appointment will always blow my mind.

Entering the process of finding your first therapist can feel like you've just decided to go to outer space. Where on Earth do you start? Sure, you know it's possible to be successful in therapy, because people on TV, in movies, and on social media have given at least a hint of insight. Their experiences seem interesting and possibly doable. But what's the first step for your own journey?

Who Am I to Say So?

If we were to rewind the tapes to my own very first therapy session as a client, you would find I was a similar giant ball of nerves, most likely stress sweating. And probably trying to find a way to back out of the whole thing.

The whole process leading up to my very first therapy session was truly a doozy. In my daily life, I had gotten increasingly uncomfortable on a day-to-day basis. Dodging imagined germs in my environment became exhausting, as did overthinking every social interaction that I found myself in. Let's not even talk about the panic attacks I had at rock climbing competitions that had me paralyzed and stuck to the climbing wall! Sleep was not a friend of mine as my anxieties hit me with a double whammy: first making me replay each awkward conversation of the day, then forcing me to relive any recent anxious thought (and there were many of these available to pick from) in the form of regular nightmares. After going through far too much of this, I mentally accepted this notion: *Okay, fine—maybe I could use the help of a professional.*

I had no idea how to go about actually finding a therapist (spoiler alert: my mom did that for me), and I found myself really confused about how to navigate the therapeutic relationship once I got started. Once I finally found someone, I had a terrible first experience with therapy. My therapist basically just wrote some tips on how to have conversations with other people on a Post-it note that promptly went in the trash. I left that experience feeling defeated and misunderstood, bound to believe that therapy was useless for the next few years until I decided to give it another go.

Thankfully, the therapy experiences I had after that first flop were helpful—so much so that I became fascinated by psychology and mental health on a professional level. I graduated with a B.A. in Psychology from Chapman University and later with my M.A. in Counseling Psychology from the University of San Francisco after a brief dabble working in human resources. (My undergraduate 60-year-old professor and academic advisor with dyed purple hair had told me the only way

I would be financially secure as a therapist would be to marry an old rich guy and wait for him to die. Safe to say that scared me into trying a more stable job, but a measly three years of facing the drudgery of the 9-to-5 corporate life inspired me to take a gamble at being a broke but fulfilled therapist anyway.) I've now had the honor of working with kids, teens, adults, and couples since starting my career as a therapist in 2022—and finding financial stability.

Since then, I have been consistently reminded by my new clients how complicated and confusing getting into therapy can be, no matter what situation you're in when you start. The majority of my clients right now are either immigrants or first-generation Americans who have pushed past cultural stigmas to make it into therapy. Many are the first of their family to ever access a mental healthcare service.

All of my clients, along with anyone who has seen a therapist, have bravely navigated the same daunting first steps to starting therapy that I did. I've heard tales about battling insurance companies, been asked what type of mental health service is best for certain issues, and have listened to clients whispering on the other end of the line so that their family members don't learn that they're seeing a therapist. If I had a dollar for every time I've explained the ins and outs of how to start therapy, I'd be rich enough to pay for everybody's therapy!

That's a mission I truly wish I could deliver, but alas I'm still embodying the broke-but-fulfilled therapist role. So instead, I'm offering this book. I truly believe that the world would be a better place if more people went to therapy. Society can be isolating these days, especially after the COVID pandemic in 2020, and it can be a relief to know there is at least one person in your corner who is committed to supporting you and your mental health.

Who Are You and How Can I Help?

Whoever you are, here I am, raising my imaginary glass to you for picking up this book. My hope is to empower you to take the first steps towards starting therapy, and to help you bust through any of those pesky walls that are currently in the way. By now you may have realized that there is an area of your life that could be tweaked for the better (if not a few areas). After reading the following chapters I'm optimistic you'll be able to easily navigate the work of figuring out your needs for therapy, finding a therapist that meets all your requirements, and entering that first session with confidence.

But I have a second hope for this book, too. Maybe you're ready for therapy, but there are barriers to starting sessions that you just can't overcome right now. Perhaps, after doing the math, checking your health coverage, and reaching out about fees, you are still not able to find a provider that meets your financial needs. Or you may have a work schedule that simply does not allow you to take time off for therapy appointments. Even with telehealth available, maybe there are no therapists in your rural area, and service is not stable enough to have a full one-hour conversation over phone or video call. Although this book is not meant to be a replacement for therapy, it may be helpful in becoming better prepared for when circumstances do allow you to take the plunge and move forward with therapy.

This book will also serve as a wading pool for anyone who is simply curious about mental health services in general and looking to just dip their toes in the water. It can be difficult to know where to start for those of us who don't have friends, family members, or mentors who have navigated mental health services. The process can be overwhelming without having any guidance or knowing what to expect. If this sounds like you, I'm optimistic that you'll finish this book with a clearer picture of next steps.

A secret ulterior motive in writing this book is also that I could have greatly benefited from such a resource in graduate school and at the very start of my career. Graduate students learning to be therapists are often surprised that the graduate school classes tend to not focus too much on the technical skills for what to actually do once you're sitting with your first client as a new therapist. While the rest of the curriculum boosts therapists-to-be in psychological knowledge and general soft skills needed for the job, it's hard to fully prepare anyone on how to be a therapist before you're in the therapist's seat. This means basically having to dive into the deep end without a floatie. Either that, or you'll see tons of training events available, but you need to sell an organ to be able to afford it as a student or new grad.

So, if you're a new therapist and nervous about that first session with a client and want to feel more prepared, this book can be a great tool to bolster your clinical skills. It's also a way to understand how your first clients might feel as they join the physical or virtual therapy space with you. We often hear that we should "meet our clients where they are," but sometimes it's hard to know where that is. So the topics covered in the following chapters might uncover something new to consider in understanding just where clients are when we first meet.

So, How Do You Use This Book?

Before we get into the meat and potatoes of areas to consider prior to starting therapy, I want to explain how this book is put together and how you might use it. Understanding how my (and many other therapists') work starts may help illustrate that.

The moment I sit down with a new client is the moment that the *assessment phase* begins. I'm starting from scratch in understanding this client's life, so we take a comprehensive, big-picture approach before zeroing in on any specific problems that emerge. Even if a new client has a sense of what they need, this "get to know you" phase is still important. The following chapters mimic the assessment phase that I complete with all new clients. We'll start with looking at the big picture in Section I, then cover lifestyle factors in Section II, mindset in Section III, and end with how to actually start and engage in therapy in Section IV.

That being said, there are a few different ways to approach this book. The most traditional way, of course, would be to go through the whole book from cover to cover, page by page. This approach could work for anybody, regardless of where you are in the process of starting therapy or how much knowledge you have about the therapeutic process.

Each chapter provides information on mental health topics (in therapist lingo we call this *psychoeducation*) and includes worksheets to help assess yourself in each topic (also known as *building awareness*). You'll see I've also sprinkled in therapeutic terminology like *assessment phase*, *psychoeducation*, and *building awareness* to help pull back the curtain on a therapist's mindframe and demystify some of the therapeutic process for you.

You can also use this book as an active guide if that suits your needs better at this time. Don't worry—as the author, I won't be offended if you jump right to the section that you think is the most relevant. Maybe one topic stands out to you today, but another chapter will call your name next month. You don't need to read the whole book in one sitting. Feel free to take a pause when you need to and revisit relevant topics as needed. You might find that different parts of this book resonate with you more when you revisit them in different stages of your life, and some parts might not feel applicable right now. The challenge, and beauty, of life is that change occurs constantly, so my aim in writing this book was to provide a comprehensive tool that includes every topic I could imagine to be relevant, and can adapt to your current situation.

Lastly, if you're really in a pinch, you can skip ahead right to the exercises. I imagine this approach to be helpful if you already have that first session with a therapist scheduled for tomorrow and want to be able to quickly identify themes to work on in therapy. The rest of the book will be right here waiting for you whenever you may need it.

Now that you have some clarity on how to use this book, it's time to get out your utensils for the meat and potatoes.

i didn't want to
either

Chapter 1

Mapping Your Emotional Landscape

Remember when I mentioned I'd be dropping in terms like *building awareness* in the Introduction? I think now is as good a time as any to start fleshing out more of this therapy lingo, starting with this exact term.

Half the battle of being in therapy is what therapists refer to as *building awareness*. For instance, maybe you discover that a filling meal in the morning is a non-negotiable thing you need to kick-start your day. Or perhaps you learn that you work better in the office when you wear noise-canceling headphones. And connecting the dots between your dust allergy and your constant bad mood in older buildings? These all fall under the umbrella of *building awareness*.

When your emotional, physical, and mental awareness increases, you'll be able to make more informed choices, which often results in improved mental health. You may be wondering, "All right, this sounds great but how the heck do I build awareness if that's half the battle?" A great starting place for building awareness is to create a map of your emotional landscape.

Fear not; building an emotional landscape is not as daunting or vague as it sounds. The best way I've heard this concept explained is to imagine that there are a bunch of holes in the floor of your living room. Obviously it would be great to repair the holes, but you don't have the tools for that yet. You also know that accidentally falling through the holes when you're trying to walk around would not feel great. So we need to map out the holes and locate the safely walkable surfaces to help you move around without taking an unexpected tumble. This is what we'll be doing in this chapter. We'll do a walk-through of your emotions to identify which ones might be holes and which ones are sturdy hardwood.

To map your current emotional landscape, we'll start with defining the specific emotions that are creating the holes in your floor. Sometimes all we know is that we're either feeling generally "good" or "bad" in a certain circumstance. Pinpointing that specific type of "good" or "bad" helps us better understand ourselves and the situation at hand. From there, we can use some detective skills and put the magnifying glass on the factors that correlate with those emotions.

Once we've gathered all the data around your emotions and the corresponding stimuli, you can be better prepared for the next time you run into them. I'll walk you through some skills that should help equip you to face the tougher emotions no matter what they are. I'll also provide you with the tools to create your own strategy if you'd like to make a more situation-specific plan of action. From there, it will be time for you to practice navigating your emotional landscape—but this time with the help of your handy dandy new map.

Can You Identify Your Emotions?

The wheel of emotions is a fantastic tool originally created by Dr. Gloria Willcox for breaking down primary emotions into specific descriptors (Wilcox, 1982). You can find all the cute and aesthetically-pleasing versions of this wheel through a quick search online.

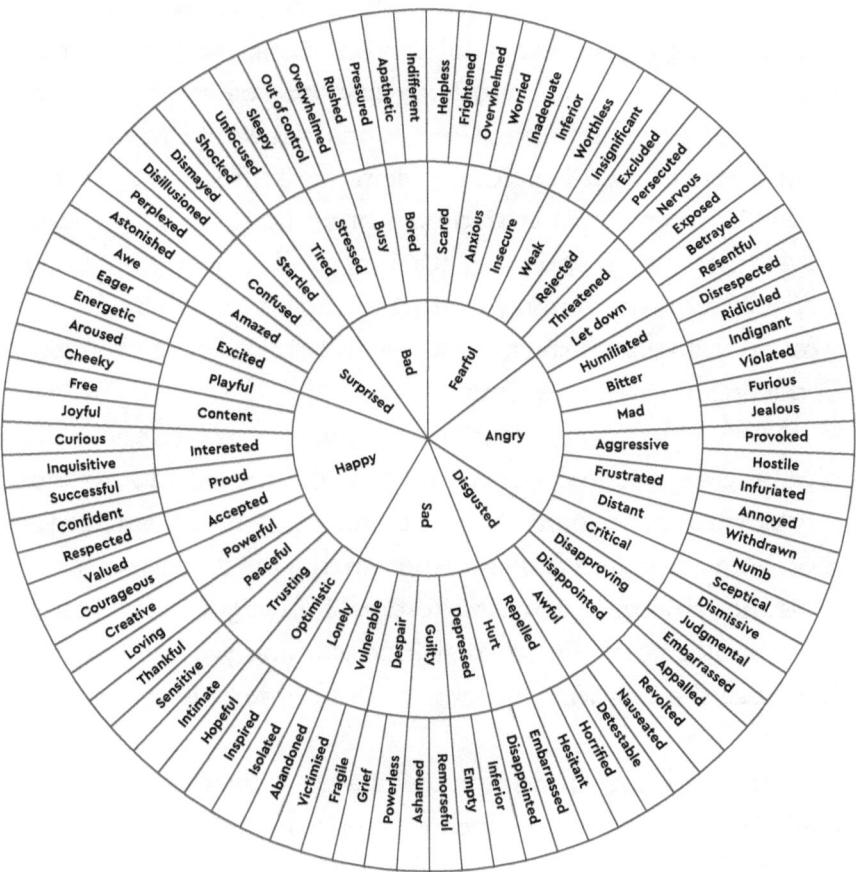

Take a minute to review the wheel above. What stood out to you as you looked through it? I've found that my clients are typically quick to identify the negative emotions. That makes sense, of course, because those are the ones that we're all often trying to move away from. You may have done the same, already envisioning the last time you felt those particular emotions as you went through the list. Make sure you don't entirely skip over the positive emotions, though.

Your emotional landscape includes the whole gamut—from the bright and shiny emotions to the dark and dreary ones. In only focusing on the less palatable emotions, you're encouraging your brain to only seek those emotions as you go through your day. By highlighting the emotions you want to experience more frequently, and exploring them more throughout the rest of this chapter, you're setting your brain up to be on the lookout for pleasant experiences. It's akin to when you think about a specific type of car and you start seeing it everywhere. Do you want to train your brain to spot the rusted clunkers on the road or the flashy new sports cars?

An effective way to identify the wider range of emotions you regularly experience is to mentally walk through an average day or week in your life. From the moment you wake up to the moment you drift off to sleep, what are the most common emotions that emerge in your day-to-day life? I suggest that you go in chronological order the first time you analyze your routine. Consider the following questions and perhaps let your mind marinate on it.

Start with the moment you wake up—how do you usually feel? Did your dreams or lack thereof result in any particular feeling? Then, what does your morning usually look like? Is it slow and relaxed or are you in a race to get out the door? Does your morning commute (or transition into work or school) excite you or infuriate you? What emotional impact do your responsibilities have on you throughout the day? What is your emotion-al state leading up to mid-day meals, during eating, and while getting back to your day afterwards? Or if you skip meals, what are the consequences to your mood? What is your energy like in the latter half of the day, and what is your mindset as you settle back home or into your evening activities? What feelings do you carry with you as you prepare for bed and sleep?

I want to encourage you to be as specific as possible in dis-secting the emotions that come up for you. Part of the genius of the wheel of emotions lies in the linguistic relativity hypothesis, which is a fancy way to say we can't fully understand something until we know the name for it. So in narrowing down the larger feeling to a more specific descriptor, you'll be able to get more in tune with the emotions that are present in your daily life.

EXERCISE 1.1 EMOTIONS

As you look through the different layers of emotions, find the ones that are most apparent in your day-to-day life. List out the correlating emotions in the second and third rings of the feelings wheel that resonate with you.

Happy:
Surprised:
Bad:
Fearful:
Angry:
Disgusted:
Sad:

Looking at your list, circle the three emotions that you experi-ence most frequently. If you'd like, let these emotions be your focus throughout the rest of this chapter.

Correlating Factors

After reflecting on your frequently experienced emotions, the next step is to examine the circumstances in which they occurred. I like to refer to the elements in these situations as *correlating factors*. You can think of correlating factors as the cousin to what pop culture prescribes as "triggers." Whereas triggers have a cause-and-effect relationship with the resulting consequence, and are thought to initiate that response one hundred percent of the time, correlating factors are more loosely associated.

For example, the weather is a common correlating factor for many people's emotions. Gloomy weather in particular. Dark clouds are often associated with lower mood, but does that mean the incoming storm guarantees a negative emotional response? Not necessarily. The relationship between this weather and the resulting emotions might be more of a ratio than an absolute certainty. Maybe you feel down in the dumps 80 percent of the time when the sky is gray, neutral 5 percent of the time, and absolutely ecstatic that you get a reprieve from the hot sun and mosquitoes the remaining 15 percent of the time.

By isolating these factors as individual contributors to the corresponding emotions, we're actually giving you more control. Using "triggers" as a comparison once again, we can see how the cause-and-effect scenario gives the trigger all the power, reducing you down to a predictable reaction. But you are so much more than that. You are a person navigating various events and stimuli in each moment of your existence. Identifying the factors that have the most impact on your emotions will ultimately allow you to make a game plan and take control of your emotional response.

EXERCISE 1.2 EMOTIONAL CORRELATIONS

Referencing the emotions you listed above, write down the factors that you think may be correlated with when you experience these emotions.

Emotion:
Likely correlating factors:
How often do these factors lead to this emotion?
Always / Usually / Sometimes / Rarely

Which Layers Do You Live In?

As humans, we have more similarities to jawbreakers than you might think. I like to visualize our existence as an individual wrapped in various layers that add unique color and flavor to how we view life. These various layers range from personally intimate to immediate family and to the external world. The core of the jawbreaker is, well, you! The jawbreaker expands from the middle—the nucleus being your mind—to the different surrounding layers that influence your existence.

A common assumption is that the map for our emotional landscape should stay primarily focused on the central flavor at the heart of the jawbreaker. This is where your needs, ego, beliefs, values, skills, and habits live. And to be fair, the center of your mind is a pretty big player! Without that middle flavor, none of the other layers could have been added. We would be remiss, however, to not take into account how the "self" is impacted by external influences, too.

The closest few layers surrounding your mind can be categorized as the *micro environment*, which expands to include the

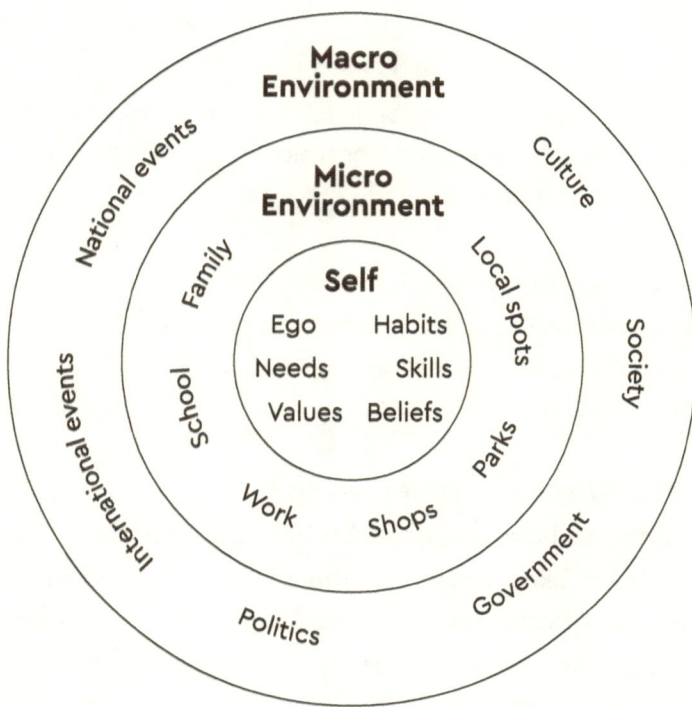

external factors that we are actively involved in. The first micro environment that you're ever exposed to, and arguably the most influential (I'm looking at you, Freud), is the family unit. As you go through life, you're likely exposed to additional micro environments such as friends' family units, schools, and workplaces. Your favorite local restaurant, the community library, and your often-frequented grocery stores also fall under this category.

Some of these elements are interconnected, while others stand alone. For example, our caregivers have a lot of sway over how we initially view the world. The narratives that we pick up from our parents and guardians can create biased interpretations of other environments that we find ourselves in. If your dad is the world's greatest fan of hot sauce, you're likely to view hot sauce as a very important condiment. Finding a void of hot sauce at friends' houses, restaurants, and the school cafeteria may cause confusion, anger, or even shame.

Thoughts like, *What is wrong with these people?* Or even worse feelings, like *What is wrong with me that I value something no one else cares about?*, can emerge. You might cope by swearing off hot sauce and distancing yourself from your dad, or creating a secret stash of to-go hot sauces for when you're out and about. Even such a small and silly example can highlight the impact that our immediate micro environment can have on our minds.

So, what larger layer is your micro environment nestled in? If you look past these most immediate local environments, you'll find yourself further situated in your *macro environment*. This includes politics and governmental policies on the state and national level, societal expectations, and overarching culture. Therapists often see an influx of clients, for example, during presidential elections and cultural events. (Hello, Thanksgiving family conflicts!) Although we're not directly "interacting" with these larger systems, they still have influence over our well-being.

As you read through the descriptions of the various layers, were you able to pinpoint any specific environments or factors that are present in your unique jawbreaker? Take some time to reflect on which layers interact with each other and which ones are independent. Do some layers have a stronger color or flavor than others? Are there any positive layers that neutralize the less pleasant ones?

Each layer interacts with the other, which is why building awareness in this arena can provide clarity. Parts of your outer layers may be influencing your inner self, mingling with the holes or walkable surface of your metaphorical living room floor. We gain a little more control once we're able to identify these factors because it makes deciding the next step of action that much easier.

EXERCISE 1.3 EMOTIONAL INFLUENCERS

In reflecting on the layers and environments that we just learned about, which ones stand out to you? Think about each layer and which aspect of the layer impacts you the most.

Self:
Microenvironment:
Macroenvironment:

In reviewing your reflection, which layer seems to have the strongest influence on your daily emotional state right now?

How Do We Prepare for Emotional Events?

Hopefully, the map for your emotional landscape is now looking a little more clear, making it possible to then set up coping skills for the emotions and factors that are relevant to your unique circumstance. The natural human instinct is typically to try to avoid uncomfortable factors altogether. However, you might be doing yourself a disservice by focusing on avoidance rather than preparation. In returning to the living room floor metaphor, you're more than likely going to step into the holes in the floor every once in a while, but the right preparations will ease the fall and aid you in bouncing back faster.

To aid in this, *cognitive defusion* is a fantastic first skill to practice. This clinical-sounding term refers to the ability to look at your thoughts before acting on them. Cognitive defusion is universal in that it can apply to any emotion. Thinking about how your husband loaded the dishwasher this morning and feeling irritated? Take a breath and decide if the lecture you're practicing in your mind is the best course of action. Feeling sad about the local pandas being transferred to a different zoo? Acknowledge the feeling and decide how long you're wanting to hold onto the sadness before letting it go.

Developing the ability to take a step back from your emotions allows you the clarity on how to best move forward. If stepping back from the thoughts and emotions weren't enough to help them move through you, this could mean you need to gain enough space to select an effective additional coping skill. Here are some of my favorite go-tos, which we'll explore more in later chapters: using grounding skills, engaging in physical exercise, practicing gratitude, and journaling.

Implementing *protective factors* can also help you curb negative emotions and boost the positive ones. You can think of these as the personal bodyguards to your emotions—an extra barrier of protection for your mental health. Protective factors can include things like strong family or social support, active practice of self-care, or spending personal time intentionally (relaxing or engaging in hobbies that give you joy). Self-sabotaging your important project is a little bit tougher to do when you have an accountability buddy to check in with, for example, just as engaging in your weekly Tuesday painting session can keep you from sinking deeper into a dark emotional hole. Consciously incorporating these factors into your life essentially creates a buffer zone between you and the more difficult emotions you may encounter.

Don't forget to think about the positive emotions in your landscape, too! Your positive and neutral emotions are the solid floor of your emotional landscape that we want to utilize regularly and eventually extend. Think of these as your emotional safety net. Practicing mindfulness can help you be immersed in the nice moments. Try to catch yourself when you're feeling good, or even just content, and lean into it. Notice the cool breeze on your skin, the smell of your morning coffee, or the satisfaction of crossing something off your to-do list. Practicing mindfulness even five minutes a day can lead to a brain structure that is more likely to recognize the good things that surround you while also having an easier time pausing and emotionally regulating in moments of difficulty.

EXERCISE 1.4 EMOTIONAL TOOLKIT

Now that you've identified your emotions, correlating factors, and personal layers, it's time to create your personalized emotional toolkit. Using cognitive defusion and protective factors, develop your action plan.

Part A: Cognitive Defusion Practice

Choose one emotion from Exercise 1.1 that you'd like to practice stepping back from. Write out a recent situation where you experienced this emotion.

Situation:
The thoughts that came up:

Now, rewrite those thoughts as if you're observing them from the outside (e.g., "I'm having the thought that...").

Reframed thoughts:

Part B: Your Protective Factor Inventory

List three protective factors you currently have in your life.

Building Awareness

As we close this chapter, I'd like to invite you to reflect on what we've discussed thus far. Which emotions, factors, and layers jumped out at you when thinking about your life? If even only one thing comes to mind, then congratulations, you're starting to build awareness! Just as we benefit from naming concepts to understand them, we can move forward in growth by better understanding ourselves.

I want to also commend you for pushing through any dis-comfort you experienced through this first chapter. Sometimes getting to know ourselves can be uncomfortable, with the hab-it of avoiding intimacy or vulnerability with ourselves being a protective shield. Moving forward into the unknown without that shield is scary.

Try to keep your building-awareness-eyes open and your shield down as we continue onto the next few chapters. The more data we gather on your current state of mind, the more positive progress we'll be able to implement.

Chapter 2

Recognizing Patterns and Habits

In the first chapter, we reviewed your emotional landscape. Emotions are a huge part of what makes humans, well, human! But are emotions the main reason we seek therapy? I'm not so convinced. Sometimes we seek a therapist's help when our feelings are an indicator that something larger is amiss in terms of how we are behaving and operating day to day. My belief about human nature is that many of our actions—and therefore our emotional responses following those actions—can be boiled down into a series of behavior patterns. So while we certainly want to focus on the emotions popping up in our lives, we should also do some detective work to uncover any cycles of behavior that could be negatively impacting our emotions.

When working with clients, my brain is always looking for patterns and habits that the client engages in, either consciously or subconsciously. I mention habits and patterns separately because, although they are often used interchangeably, they are slightly different concepts. Habits are like the square to a pattern's rectangle; squares are technically categorized as a type of rectangle but are also seen as distinct shapes, too. So habits are indeed patterns, but are their own set of conditions, as well.

Both patterns and habits can occur within various aspects of our lives, such as inside of relationships, work, and leisure time. The main difference between overarching patterns of behavior and habits is intentionality. Patterns generally happen whether you intend for them to or not. They also can happen on a more sporadic basis. Maybe you tend to snack on popcorn on rainy days, or watch the same classic holiday movies as soon as November hits. A pattern I'm known for is whipping up a batch of cardamom buns any time I notice a few hours of free time in my schedule.

Patterns seem to "happen when they happen," so to speak, without much deliberate intentionality. Habits, on the other hand, are associated with specific tasks that are attempted or executed on a more regular and predictable basis. I use the word *attempted* to highlight the fact that there is intention in wanting to perform the action, and to point out that sometimes we can fall short on completing habits despite our best intentions. Habits include brushing our teeth twice a day, exercising three times a week, or choosing a specific playlist for the commute home from work.

When I zero in on the patterns and habits that emerge in discussions with my clients, I like to organize them into two categories: effective or ineffective. While ineffective actions may be blocking or impeding us in some way, effective ones add to our lives or keep things going smoothly. From there, we find a way to address ineffective patterns and continue, or even boost, effective patterns. Keep in mind that this process is very binary thinking for the sake of simplicity, since you're in the early stage of this process. You may be able to examine repeated behaviors in more detail further along your journey.

The terms *effective* and *ineffective* also don't equate to "good" or "bad." I find that many of us feel shame when we label behaviors as "bad." So, instead, let's determine what's working for you and what isn't. The quality of the habit also depends on the conditions that it's occurring within. A behavior that was effective in your past, and under different circumstances, might be standing in your way now.

Maybe your morning coffee ritual gave you stability and something to look forward to in your early career, for example. It was effective in that it added value to your typical day, or was at least a neutral task on a rough one. Let's say now you've started a new job with a longer commute, and you have to rush through your morning routine. If taking time to make a perfectly-crafted latte is creating stress and putting you in a bad mood, perhaps this action has become ineffective.

Now, the goal is not necessarily to eliminate every ineffective pattern or habit taking place in your life. Your habits and patterns are also in a constant state of change just like life itself, so keeping up with all the continuous shifts would take an enormous amount of time and energy. The key instead is to strike a balance. We'll first tune into your ineffective habits and patterns, then look at the effective ones.

Recognizing Ineffective Patterns and Habits

Ineffective patterns and habits often end up taking a toll on your mental health, either in the moment or later on down the road.

Luckily, ineffective patterns and habits both share the same indicators. The most obvious of the indicators being a glaringly, in-your-face negative reaction. This could look like an internal feeling such as a queasy gut reaction after consuming a third black coffee instead of water, or an external indicator like another person's frown in response to your witty yet possibly ill-timed sarcastic comment. These indicators tend to be immediate, making it easy to identify the anteceding event—be it pattern or habit—that resulted in a negative shift.

Other indicators can be a little more vague and not so immediately clear. This makes pinpointing the cause a bit harder, but not impossible. Look for general emotional discomfort, feeling "stuck" and having difficulty making progress, or a lingering sense of being unfulfilled. Do any of these resonate with you? If so, I have two helpful methods for discovering the ineffective habit or pattern. One technique is a bit passive (I love a good activity that can be done from the couch!), while the other is more active.

The first way to retroactively assess your patterns and habits is similar to how I picture the inner workings of Sherlock Holmes's mind: reviewing the case and highlighting possible clues. Questions that may help bring the clues to light are:

- Did anything happen around the same time that I started to feel this way?

- Last time I felt this way, what was going on in my life?

- When these feelings were absent in my life, was I doing anything differently than I am now?

Moving your answers from your mind onto paper may also help you see or understand the data better. I frequently encourage my clients to make lists, timelines, or even elaborate detective-like spiderwebs of strings on a bulletin board of clues if that might be helpful in better understanding the information you're processing.

The second method is to experiment. I use the word *experiment* on purpose—I think it's a great way to invite people to engage in lifestyle or mental health changes in a way that allows for curiosity, playfulness, and reduced pressure. The purpose of the experiment is to collect data that helps us gain more understanding of what we're going through. (See how *building awareness* pops up all the time in the therapy world?) If you feel unmotivated to go on your daily run, try cycling or pilates for a week and see if that has any impact on your mood. Observe any differences in your ability to focus and feel productive if you try to work at a different desk or cafe to address your current mental block in workflow.

The best part about experiments is that they're noncommittal. Did you find out that a slower-paced exercise routine better fits your lifestyle these days? Great, now you can turn that experiment into a habit! But if the change of scenery didn't lessen your feeling stuck at work, at least you got to take in a new view and cross off that category from your detective list of suspects. As the data rolls in, you'll be able to make the appropriate adjustments and bask in the positive outcome that results.

EXERCISE 2.1 PATTERN EXPERIMENTATION

Put the clues together. Think about one of the emotions from the previous chapter and answer the following questions to see if any patterns emerge.

- When was the last time you felt this way?
- What environments were you in when you've felt this way before?
- Were there any behaviors or activities that you're doing now that you did last time you felt this way, or anything you did when you were feeling better that is absent in your life now?

Experiment brainstorm. Come up with a few short-term experiments that would be easy to commit to over the next few weeks or so. Some examples are:

- *I can try meal prepping on Sunday so I'm not rushing to figure out food during the week.*
- *Since my boss usually asks for a last-minute meeting on Mondays to discuss my goals for the week, I'll see if sending her an update email in the morning can make that connection more intentional for my work flow.*
- *I'm going to turn my phone on airplane mode when I get home so I don't get distracted and doom scroll until I sleep.*

Recognizing Effective Patterns and Habits

Let's flip the script and talk about effective habits and patterns. Similar to ineffective habits and patterns, those that are effective also share a lot of the same indicators. So we're going to play "Opposite Day" with all those indicators we discussed for the ineffective ones.

Take a moment to reflect on those little bursts of joy you've experienced lately. Maybe it's a sparkle of happiness you feel when you bite into your favorite mid-morning snack (yum, chocolate croissant!), or the warm fuzzies you get when your boss finally notices your impeccable attention to detail. How about that nice glimmer when a new friendship starts to blossom because you've been bravely putting yourself out there? These positive reactions are quick indicators for your effective habits.

The "Opposite Day" approach applies to the bigger, more vague indicators, too. Instead of feeling stuck in a rut, you might notice a general sense of forward momentum. Like your life has suddenly gained a Mario-Kart-style boost. You might notice feeling energized, motivated, fulfilled, productive, or generally just a little more relaxed. These are all fantastic signs that you've got some effective patterns and habits well-established in the foundation of your day-to-day routines. Also, don't underestimate the power of just being content. In a world that capitalizes on extreme highs and dramatic lows, finding satisfaction by coasting on the midline is a skill often overlooked.

Now, here's a funny thing: our brains are much more attuned to recognize the effective habits and patterns attributed to positive reactions than the ineffective ones. It's as if our brains have a built-in radar for finding anything in the "feel-good" category. We are often intentional in implementing new effective habits and patterns in anticipation of the positive consequence (like, "Hey, I heard that a celery juice cleanse is great for digestive health."), which makes it easier to notice and feel gratitude for it. ("Wow I feel healthier and happier after trying that celery juice cleanse!") We're also generally more open to understanding our positive experiences because there's less risk involved. Digging into our ineffective habits and patterns to discover that a favorite guilty pleasure is the culprit feels more scary and less enticing to be aware of. Hence the phrase "ignorance is bliss."

But don't worry if the source of your positive vibes doesn't immediately volunteer itself. Just because it's easier to pinpoint the starting effective habit doesn't mean you'll always recognize it from the get-go. As when finding your ineffective habits and patterns, try to zoom into the specific circumstances associated with the positive indicators. Retroactively analyze what was going on in times where you've felt elevated and see if there are any common actions that come to your awareness.

The fun part about identifying your effective habits and patterns is deciding how to keep them up. You can continue them as they are, or amp them even more! Take a moment to sit with positive emotions when they show up. That way, you can feel the full presence of the positive reaction and solidify that happy moment to memory. Staying aware of the pleasant actions and emotions can help balance out the not-so-great ones while we're still working on changing them.

EXERCISE 2.2 PATTERN RECOGNITION

Think about the last time you felt energized, productive, or genuinely content.

When did this happen?

What were you doing that day/week?
List three to four specific activities.

What patterns do you notice?
Note things that apply to your effective moments.

- Specific time of day

- Certain people around you
- Physical activity level
- Sleep/eating routine
- Environment/location
- Work/life balance

How can you amplify these? Choose one or two effective patterns to do more of this week.

How to Change Ineffective Patterns and Habits

Once you've identified the ineffective habits and patterns that are holding you back, the next step is to modify the ones that you feel ready to work on. This is where things may get tricky, potentially even frustrating, but the process can be highly empowering once you make it to the other side. (It is possibly also where a therapist can help.) No matter what, I want to remind you to practice self-compassion and patience with yourself as you implement and maintain new patterns and habits. You might find yourself slipping into past ineffective habits and patterns—and that is to be expected! The goal is to reduce the frequency and intensity of the current ineffective ones and increase the new effective alternatives.

Understanding the habit loop is a great starting place for tackling habit (and pattern) changes. A habit loop—a concept first introduced by Charles Duhigg in *The Power of Habit* (2013)—can be boiled down to three main components:

1. a cue that triggers a habit,
2. the habit itself, and
3. the reward that you gain from the habit.

I find that this loop applies equally to patterns of behavior as well. Once you identify the cue and the reward, you can get creative in choosing a new habit or pattern. For example, mindful breathing exercises are a common swap for smoking because both smoking and mindful breathing can be used after a stress cue and can result in the reward of decreased stress.

Once a new action is identified, then we can set it into motion! You're probably not going to be able to completely change your habits and patterns overnight, so don't be too hard on yourself at the start. Progress may look like a slow ramp-up. The ineffective habits and patterns will decrease over time just as the effective ones increase.

There are several tips and tricks I like to share with clients who are trying to implement new, effective habits and patterns. The most actionable advice is to implement *environmental design*. Do you have a pattern of being snappy to others in the morning after a bad night's rest? Think about any decor or joyful morning activity that you can bring into your life to better support a consistent improved mood in the morning, no matter the previous night's sleep conditions, and therefore curb the temptation to be snappy at the first person you see. If you're thinking of replacing doom scrolling on social media to reading, perhaps replacing your social media apps with an e-reading app will encourage you to follow through with your goal.

I also encourage clients to be intentional and to start small. This is a great two-for-one punch. Setting an intention and checking in with yourself on that intention keeps your mind focused and cognizant of the change you're trying to make. Starting small sets you up for success in tweaking your habits and patterns by making it more approachable. We want to keep up the momentum of the change, so hitting the ground running might result in burnout rather than long-term change.

Instead of expecting an overnight transformation from being grouchy throughout the day to a world-renowned optimist, it might be a better idea to set a routine morning intention to practice gratitude and assume positive intent from others for as long as you can that day. Some days your positivity might last until the afternoon, or others you might be disrupted by the first business meeting of the day. That's okay. Just keep practicing and expanding the parameters when you're comfortable.

EXERCISE 2.3 HABIT LOOPS

Create a habit loop swap by choosing a habit/pattern from Exercise 2.1 to work on.

Step 1: Identify the Cue
What typically happens right before this habit? (Stress, boredom, specific time, location, emotion)

Step 2: Identify the Reward
What do you get from this habit? (Stress relief, entertainment, avoidance, comfort, etc.)

Step 3: Design Your Swap
What new habit could give you the same reward when you encounter the same cue?

Step 4: Environmental Design
What one change can you make to your environment to support this new habit?

Step 5: Start Small
What's the smallest version of this new habit you could try for just one week?

Targeting Habits and Patterns

Once you've made a swap or phased out an ineffective habit or pattern, make sure to stay vigilant. (In less of a Batman kind of way, but more of an active birdwatching style.) Mark your calendar or set a reminder every couple of months to self-assess your current patterns and habits. You can even make note of your top effective and ineffective ones. This way, you can stay aware of those that impact you the most and check the ratio to see if they're balanced.

If the equilibrium is off, dabble in some experiments to see what might need to be changed. Don't forget to be creative and have fun in the process. Change can be exciting and invigorating. If you're needing some more encouragement, you can lean into the strengths and resources we discuss in the next chapter to help with targeting your habits and patterns.

Chapter 3

Identifying Your Strengths and Resources

Have you seen those graphs that indicate progress? You know, the ones that show what progress ideally looks like versus the reality of how progress happens? The idealized version is usually a beautiful line graph with a smooth and steady upward trajectory, because we all likely hope that our energy and effort are equally rewarded with predictable improvement. The reality, however, can be depicted as a line that looks like your favorite roller coaster, full ups, downs, and loopty-loops. While the drops on an amusement ride are thrilling, the drops on the path to meeting your mental health goals might be less fun.

Having a secure safety net in place can help with any drops that will naturally occur throughout your self-improvement process. To facilitate this, at the start of therapy, I like to highlight any strengths and resources that my clients already have set up in their lives. This includes having friends who can be there for you when you're feeling down, engaging in hobbies that bring you joy, and an optimistic mindset. Even having access to transportation or the Internet can be life-changing resources.

Building up these resources will help whenever you're feeling a bit out of your depths while you're trying to build up new skills and tackle the tough parts of your psyche, because you can lean on the good that already exists. The best part of cataloging your strengths and resources ahead of time is that you reduce the effort needed later on down the road when your mental energy is already being directed toward other life changes. You can tap into your reserves, so to speak. We'll delve into strengths first, then work our way to highlighting your resources so that we can stock up your inventory.

Summing Up Your Strengths

Strengths can be difficult to identify right off the bat because the overall category is a bit ambiguous, and personal strengths come in all sorts of shapes and sizes. For the purpose of this chapter, we'll use the umbrella term "strengths" to encapsulate the following:

Character strengths. Like your innate kindness to others, or your ability to persevere through challenges, character strengths can be intertwined with your personality or show up in your actions.

Cognitive strengths. Are you street-smart, book-smart, or maybe both? Cognitive strengths can reflect intellect, like being a computer whiz, as well as other forms of intelligence like emotional intelligence, musical intelligence, and more.

Interpersonal strengths. This is reflected in your relationships with others, from strangers to colleagues or family. Interpersonal strengths could look like being able to communicate effectively with others or to be able to anticipate the needs of people around you.

Ability Strengths. Think of a talent show—what skills do you have up your sleeve? If you can whittle a stick into art or even if you can simply boil water, you've got an ability strength.

The benefit of identifying your strengths is that then you're able to recognize how often they come into your daily life. I call this the Yellow Jeep Theory—at first you might not think that there are many yellow Jeeps driving around, but once they're in your awareness, you'll notice that yellow Jeeps are actually all around! (This is inspired by a childhood vacation where we rented a bright yellow Jeep and suddenly it seemed like they were everywhere we went.)

If you're not feeling so great right now, and that's the top focus of your mind, it's much easier to find the evidence around you that supports your negative experience. So by cataloging your strengths, we can instead redirect your mind to pay attention to them more frequently. Then as you go throughout your daily routine, you'll be able to locate the evidence that supports your confidence and mental health.

An example would be noticing your decision to give someone else your seat on the train (character strength). Then you navigate the shortcut you discovered from the train station to your office, allowing you to get to work earlier than everyone else (cognitive strength) and a fresh jump to the day. This allows you extra time at lunch to visit with a colleague you haven't seen in awhile (interpersonal). At the end of the day, you make a relaxing cup of tea and work on a puzzle (ability). If you had a bad day but were able to recognize one strength from each of the four strength subcategories throughout it, imagine how much balance could be brought to your overall mood.

If you find that your mind is immediately reacting with the thought, "But I don't have many (or any) strengths or resources," you would not be alone. This is the exact sentiment shared by many of my clients when I first broach the subject. The brain is a funny thing. Our memory recalls sad moments throughout our lives much faster when we are feeling sad. Meanwhile, pleasant memories are easier to pinpoint when we're in a happier mood. Take a moment to notice your current mood and the types of memories you're able to bring to the surface. If you are having difficulty identifying any personal strengths right now, it might be beneficial to return to this topic when you're in a better mood.

Your critical inner voice can also be acting as a barrier to discovering your hidden strengths. Pay attention to any negative self-talk telling yourself things like "Well anyone can do that," or "That's not anything special." We tend to downplay our abilities and give in to feelings of imposter syndrome. If you notice these thoughts or feelings toward any potential strengths, take a step back and inspect the strength without an emotional lens. This could give you the clarity you need to either add it to your list of strengths or to gently file it away as a possible area for growth.

Lastly (and I'm sure you're starting to see an investigation pattern here from the previous chapter), I'd recommend you to think back to a past challenge. In reframing your experience of this difficult time, ask yourself what you took away from it. Maybe getting laid off from your corporate job nudged you to take the plunge with your crafting gig, or you picked up a valuable lesson in communication through that last relationship ending. Turning lemons into lemonade can help you highlight the hidden strengths you've gained over time.

EXERCISE 3.1 STRENGTHS INVENTORY

Let's create your strengths inventory. For each category, write down one to two strengths you have. If you're struggling, think of a recent compliment someone gave you or a challenge you overcame.

> **Character Strengths:** Kindness, perseverance, honesty, humor, etc.
>
> **Cognitive Strengths:** Problem-solving, creativity, learning quickly, etc.
>
> **Interpersonal Strengths:** Listening, making others comfortable, teamwork, etc.
>
> **Ability Strengths:** Cooking, organizing, fixing things, artistic skills, etc.
>
> **Past Challenge to Hidden Strength:** Think of a difficult time you got through. What strength did you discover or develop?

Recognizing Your Resources

Resources, like strengths, provide support when needed. But unlike your strengths, resources are external to you. Although this is the forte of social workers, therapists are also likely to check your level of social, professional, and online resources. It's surprisingly easy to forget about all the resources we have available to us. We can get stuck in our own bubble, or try to "tough it out" on our own. Reaching out for external support can also feel vulnerable, which is tricky to add on to existing challenges that you're navigating, but the benefit of gaining support from those outside yourself might outweigh the potential risk.

Social Support

We will do a deeper dive on social support in Chapter 9, but I thought it would be important to touch on here, too. Social support is relatively straight-forward to assess. The main question being: how often are you interacting with others? Think about how often you're chatting with friends and family, or collaborating with colleagues. How many of these interactions are in-person, over the phone, or some other virtual means of communicating? And out of each of these modalities, which is the most fulfilling to you?

With the rise of working from home and communicating via writing rather than face-to-face, I'm seeing an increase in social isolation with my clients. If you're communicating with others regularly but still not feeling totally connected, consider switching up the way you're interacting. If texting is keeping things surface-level, schedule a call or a coffee meet-up. Even video calls can make a world of difference. Like we did in the previous chapter, the main goal here is to switch from things that are not working to one that may be a little more successful.

For personal social support, you might find that merely increasing the amount of time spent talking with others is enough to give you a boost. Inviting friends or family in to help with whatever you're dealing with isn't mandatory (although I wouldn't be opposed if you tried!), but if you're feeling particularly avoidant of disclosing any struggles to personal connections, checking out professional resources might be a better route to consider.

Professional Support

I'll explain all the various professional options in greater detail in Chapter 16, but we can do a brief overview now. Therapists, psychologists, social workers, and psychiatrists (along with psychiatric physician assistants and psychiatric mental health nurse practitioners) are all professionals who are trained to help with mental health, and are held to legal and ethical regulations. You might meet with a professional one-on-one if you're engaging in therapy, a psychological assessment, or medication management session. If you're more comfortable with group settings, group therapy, support groups, workshops, or retreats could be more your speed.

I've had plenty of clients tell me that they're more comfortable sharing the skeletons in their closet to me than to their friends or family members. I imagine that this is largely due to the fact that I have a professional interest, not personal stake, in my clients' actions. For example, I won't shame my clients for making an ineffective decision but rather would safely explore the decision and find a way to move forward appropriately. Similarly, some clients don't feel an attachment to a therapist's potential personal reactions the way they would to those from their loved ones. The possibility of dismay from a therapist might sting, but hearing the words "I'm disappointed in you" from a parent or sibling feels a lot heavier.

Comfort can also be found in knowing that professional support is contained, so to speak. Most therapy, psychological, and psychiatric appointments occur within a set timeframe. It can feel reassuring to know that vulnerability, or even the discomfort of actually *feeling* your feelings, can be over by the end of the session time. Then there's the bonus that the professional you're meeting with has likely helped others going through a similar situation as yourself, and they're qualified to teach you the skills to manage it unlike friends, family, and sketchy online gurus.

Online Support

If in-person attention sounds too intense, the Internet is at your disposal! No, I'm not going back on my word and encourage you to seek out the online gurus, but instead am suggesting that research-based apps might be worth your while. This is a great way to dip your toe into the self-care realm without committing to steep fees to work with professionals and perhaps share things you're not ready to talk about yet. There are apps and websites for general mental health and for specific areas of struggle like ADHD or anxiety.

At the very minimum, you can also always crack open YouTube to learn more about the challenges you're facing. There are tons of qualified professionals uploading videos about skills, tools, and advice for specific concerns. My disclaimer, though, is that it's easy to also fall down a rabbit hole or absorb amateur advice when watching videos or scouring the Internet about your specific situation. I would suggest putting a time limit on your research activities and sticking with professional online resources to prevent any anxious thought spiraling.

EXERCISE 3.2 RESOURCE MAPPING

Social Support. Rate each from 1 to 5.
(1 = needs work, 5 = strong support)

Family connections:
Close friendships:

Work/colleague relationships:

Community connections:

Support. Who are the top three people you could reach out to?

Professional Resources. Check any you've used or considered.
- Therapist/counselor
- Support groups
- Employee assistance program
- Religious/spiritual leader
- Life coach

Online Resources. Check any that appeal to you.
- Mental health apps
- Online therapy
- YouTube educational channels
- Online support communities
- Meditation apps

Applying Your Tools

Keeping your strengths and resources on the backburner of your mind is a skill worth building in order to be able to access them any time they're needed. Developing a mindset founded in consciousness of your strengths and resources can be done a few different ways. Mindfulness, cognitive rehearsal, and intentional goal setting are where I'd start. I'll explain each of these and you can actively practice them through the exercises at the end of this chapter.

Mindfulness

Mindfulness is a concept that can be applied to almost any therapeutic goal because it's so integral in building awareness. Mindfulness entails living in the moment occurring now, not the imagined future or thoughts of the past, and being cognizant of how the factors around you are impacting you in the real and present instance. I often suggest clients start with a mindful shower at the start of the day, taking just five minutes to notice the warmth of the water and the pressure where the water hits your skin. As you practice this skill regularly, it becomes easy to apply in other areas of your life.

Applying mindfulness to strengths and resources would entail focusing on the present moment throughout your day and keeping an eye on your emotions. As an observer, instead of getting swept away by these thoughts, analyze them to see if they incorporate your strengths or if you need any resources to help with them.

Yes, I know, this sounds mentally exhausting. What I've noticed is that mindfulness comes easily to those who intentionally practice it regularly. So if you start small with mindful showers, eating, or breathing at any point in your day, the habit can naturally bleed into the rest of your day without much mental exertion. (This is great news for anyone who, like me, wants to gain helpful new skills without grueling effort!)

Cognitive Rehearsal

Cognitive rehearsal is a similar practice, but involves the thoughts in your head rather than your sensory experience. Another fun fact about your brain is that imagined experiences can impact both it and your body just as strongly as real or tangible experiences. So a maladaptive daydream you have about totally freezing during your important presentation can get your body's stress responses revved up just as easily as if the experience were happening live. (*Maladaptive* means it's not helpful, and potentially even harmful, whereas *adaptive* describes things that are useful and valuable.) Luckily, an imagined beach day can be just as effective at calming your mind and body back down.

Using this phenomena to our advantage, we can build neural pathways by practicing skills in our mind. Cognitive rehearsing your day or a specific scenario can help with your ability to shift your mindset towards strengths and resources. Imagine going through your day and running into a problem that you frequently encounter. Now, pause the scenario in your mind and consider if any strengths or resources could apply. Then rinse and repeat as needed.

Goal Setting

In shifting our focus to the future, setting goals can help us be more intentional to incorporate our strengths, and the resources to achieve them, from the get-go. If you're wanting to go to the gym more often, leaning into your inner social butterfly strength to attend group fitness classes or having an accountability buddy would set you up for success. Or you can incorporate your knack for problem-solving with that home improvement task you've been procrastinating.

Not only will the intentionality of bringing in strengths and resources from the start help you accomplish your goals, but you might find the process to be more enjoyable, too.

EXERCISE 3.3 APPLYING YOUR TOOLS

Mindfulness Practice. Choose one daily activity where you'll practice mindfulness this week:
- Your daily shower
- Eating a meal
- Walking
- Brushing teeth

Cognitive Rehearsal. Think of an upcoming situation that feels challenging. Mentally rehearse it going well.

The situation:

Which strength you will use:

What resource might help:

Goal Setting with Strengths. Choose one goal you're working on and identify how to use your strengths/resources.

Your goal:

The strength you'll leverage:

The resource you'll tap into:

Your first small step this week:

Using Strengths to Build Confidence and Resiliency

Just like in the previous chapter, identifying and using your strengths and resources is an ongoing process. Your strengths are likely to grow and change as you do. Similarly, resources also shift throughout life. As you move to a different city, start a new job, or join new social groups, take note of any new resources that can support you when needed. In leveraging your existing strengths and resources, you're likely to find that you feel more confident and resilient to progress past challenges and make the most of your daily experiences.

EXERCISE 3.4 ONGOING TRACKING

Save this for your monthly strengths and resources check-in.

New strength(s) I've discovered:

Resource(s) I want to build:

How I used my strengths and resources this month:

Chapter 4

Assessing Readiness for Change

The previous few chapters laid the foundation for building your awareness. If you're reading this book in order, you are likely now more aware of your emotional landscape, your typical patterns and habits, and your strengths and resources. Keep these all in your back pocket as we continue forward. But before we move on to specific lifestyle factors to assess, I want to share with you one of my favorite tools as a therapist: assessing readiness for change.

As a visual person, I often share the *Stages of Change* (Prochaska & DiClemente, 1983) graphic on the following page with my clients. The Stages of Change model was developed by psychologists James Prochaska and Carlo DiClemente back in the 80s, with newer versions including a "relapse" or "burnout" stage. Although it was initially introduced as a tool to help with smoking cessation, researchers quickly realized that the model is versatile for mental health, too. It has since become a Swiss

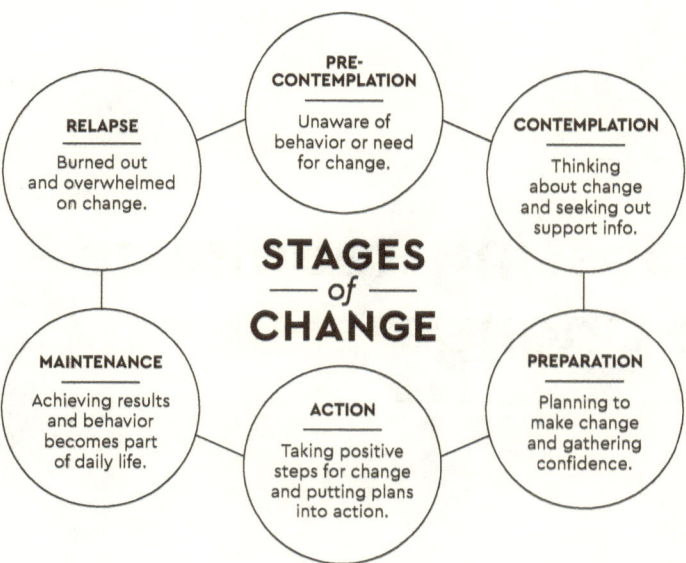

STAGES of CHANGE

PRE-CONTEMPLATION
Unaware of behavior or need for change.

CONTEMPLATION
Thinking about change and seeking out support info.

RELAPSE
Burned out and overwhelmed on change.

PREPARATION
Planning to make change and gathering confidence.

MAINTENANCE
Achieving results and behavior becomes part of daily life.

ACTION
Taking positive steps for change and putting plans into action.

Army Knife for behavioral change and a go-to for many thera-pists like myself.

As we explore the various stages of change, you might be able to recognize which stage you're sitting in with a specific desired, or undesired, change in your life. The better you under-stand each stage, the easier it will be to find that "You Are Here" marker on the metaphorical mall directory of your mind.

I want to emphasize again that change is not a linear pro-cess. Even though the model is depicted as a loop, you can ac-tually jump between the different stages instead of following them consecutively. The model is a dance of progress, not per-fection—you can take a step forward or you might find yourself taking a step backward, even steps in multiple directions. In any case, you're always in motion and learning along the way.

Understanding the different stages can prepare you to make more informed choices, and increase the chances of experienc-ing consistent forward momentum with the changes you want to put in place. You'll also be able to better recognize when a change is on the horizon but maybe should be shelved for right now. As we go through each stage, you'll likely find that you're at each one for different areas of your life, which is to be expected when you're a work in progress. (As we all are!)

Pre-Contemplation

Imagine you're lying on your longtime mattress, the one that's perfectly worn in and molded to your body. Sure, there's that pokey bump in the bottom left corner, but you've learned to lay on the right side of the bed, and actually like pulling your feet up closer to your body. There's nostalgia and comfort with this mattress. It's where you've binged your favorite comfort show on sick days, and where memories of the late-night conversations with your partner are embedded. This metaphor shows us what the pre-contemplation stage of change is like: making a change is not even on your radar.

Common sentiments we tend to have in this stage are "I am who I am; it's other people who have a problem with that," or "Why change if I've always done things this way?" In this stage, we tend to feel defensive or resort to rationalization. We're ready to go to bat for our current thoughts, feelings, and behaviors. Or, even if we do think something *might* possibly need to change, we experience feelings of helplessness, as if we're the plastic bag caught in the wind that Katy Perry so famously described in her song, "Firework."

Lastly, and quite possibly the most common feeling in this stage, is one of comfort. There's a level of security, after all, that comes with staying where you are. Often static dormancy is much more enticing than the risk of making changes that could have unknown consequences. The idiom "better the devil you know than the devil you don't" illustrates this idea, which also applies to smaller (and less maniacal) scenarios like managing with that left-hand-side mattress lump rather than accidentally replacing it with a mattress that's uncomfortable over the *entire* surface of your body.

Although it's easy to judge our pre-contemplation selves in hindsight, remember that there's nothing inherently wrong about this stage. We all start in pre-contemplation at first, and we're probably still in the pre-contemplation stage for various mystery changes at this very moment. While here in this state, your subconscious is planting the seeds for upcoming changes, which you'll become conscious of as the new sprouts break ground.

Contemplation

In the contemplation stage, you're typically sitting at a crossroads. You *could* survive with your current mattress but hey, an upgrade could be nice too. You've been thinking about sleeping in a more ergonomic, chiropractor-approved position, but your worn-in mattress feels foreign when you try to switch up your sleeping style. Now, options and choices are coming your way and you can decipher both the pros and the cons of each possibility. Essentially, the contemplation stage means that you can see that changes might be needed, but you're not quite ready to swing into action.

Hallmark feelings of the contemplation stage are ambivalence, curiosity, and inching towards acceptance: stepping out of denial and admitting that change might be needed is an uncomfortable but freeing part of the process. Your mind can see-saw between the options, tipping between reasons to make changes or reasons to keep following the same path. A side effect of this possible confusion is the need for more information. In contemplation, we often start gathering data about the current situation and the options available for moving forward. Sometimes, reviewing all the facts and figures helps your mind creep a little closer to accepting that change is necessary.

In this stage, I am a big proponent of putting your thoughts to paper. Instead of holding a tennis match in your mind, watching the ball volley between each side of the court and having to mentally keep track of the points, it's easier to physically manifest the evidence supporting each option in writing. So, I often encourage clients to write out a pros-and-cons list for each option when making decisions. There's something magical about seeing all the cards laid out on the table. It helps our brains process the decision differently than if we merely run it through our heads.

Another option I'm a fan of is more of a creative endeavor: creating your alter-ego. It's rare that we hope to be exactly the same as we are right now. So imagine who you will be in five years—a future version of your current self. What choice would this future version of yourself make? What decision would help you to get closer to becoming that version of yourself? You can start with dabbling in smaller, more comfortable changes until you get the confidence to tackle the bigger ones.

Remember that the contemplation stage exists as a space for your exploration and reflection. Be patient with yourself and don't rush the process. You're building a strong foundation for the next steps, which you'll take when you are ready. Although you might not have a firm decision made by the end of this stage, you'll have gained clarity about your current circumstances and understanding of how change might be beneficial.

EXERCISE 4.1 CHANGE EXPLORATION

Think of one change you've been considering. Use this frame-work to explore both sides.

The change I'm contemplating:
Pros of making this change:
Cons of making this change:
Pros of staying the same:
Cons of staying the same:
My future self in five years would probably:

Preparation

You're testing mattresses at the store, asking friends about their beds, and looking at reviews. The preparation stage is all about laying this groundwork before taking action. Preparation takes contemplation to the next level through strategizing and planning for the change you're ready to move forward with.

Feelings of motivation and commitment increase during preparation. You're moving from a vague idea to a more concrete plan, and ironing out the important details. You're employing information gathered in the last stage, and you're dipping your toe in the pool of something different before jumping in. My personal favorite feeling associated with the preparation stage of change is the butterflies. This is a time of excitement, anticipation, and nervousness.

Developing a thought-out plan at this point can help you see better results in the following stages. This is when you can consider specific goals, brainstorm possible obstacles, and gather resources that will help when you take action. It's tempting to skate through this stage when you're inspired to dive into the changes, but fine-tuning your plan and thinking through the tools you might need will set you up for success in the long-term. If you know you're currently in the preparation stage of a change, give yourself a pat on the back. It's courageous to shift from daydreaming about change to actively paving the way towards it.

EXERCISE 4.2 CHANGE ACTION PLAN

Building an action plan for a change you're preparing for.
> **My specific goal:**
> **Three steps I need to take to get ready:**
> **Potential obstacles I might face:**
> **Resources/people who can help:**
> **How I'll know that I'm ready to take action:**

Action

Get ready to swipe your (hypothetical) credit cards, because you're about to purchase a new mattress in the action stage of change! You have decided that it's time to take the plunge. The options between online purchase versus in-person have been weighed, and you've selected the mattress brand you want to move forward with. A new bed frame has been installed, and sheets have been washed. Your plans are migrating from paper to real-life changes.

The timeline of the action stage depends on the type of change you're making. Actions like finding a new pair of running shoes are faster and less intensive than something like renovating your kitchen. Changes to behavioral patterns or habits similarly vary in time commitment to implement. For example, remember that this model was originally created around the action of quitting smoking. Lifestyle changes like smoking cessation involves continual action that can last for weeks or months, because fighting cravings and utilizing an alternate behavior or tool are ongoing action processes. But changing the time you wake up in the morning might be as simple as setting an earlier alarm for the next day.

Being in the action phase means almost any emotion can be thrown at you—from excitement and optimism to trepidation and regret. Be prepared to go with the flow, using the work you did during contemplation and preparation to address these new challenges, and engaging in gratitude to soak in the positive moments. Consider the resources we talked about in the last chapter and if any of them could help you in making your desired change. Scientists argue that humans are the most adaptable species, meaning that *you* are adaptable, and tangible change is possible. Even if it takes time.

Implementing your change plan in small increments can help a big change feel more approachable. Practice self-compassion throughout the process, being kind and understanding to yourself if you stumble along the way, and, again, drawing from your strengths and resources as needed. You might need to adjust your plans as you go, but think of it as your GPS "recalculating" rather than coming up against a permanent traffic block. If you keep your end goal in mind, the route may change but the destination can remain the same.

No matter how long it takes, the action stage is where real transformation happens. You push past the comfort zone to experience growth and to get closer to the version of yourself that you'd like to be. Progress can feel slow, or you might be able to make changes in the blink of an eye. Once you feel settled in with the changes, then it's time to move on to the phase that will help you maintain your growth.

Maintenance

Let's say you've had your new mattress for a few months now. The novelty has worn off, and you've broken it in to be comfortable in all the right places. The maintenance stage is in full swing at this point. This is the time to keep an eye out for any possible loose threads or any growing divots in the mattress that may need to be addressed before they turn into bigger problems. Keeping the mattress in tip-top shape is the priority so that the change process doesn't have to start all over again.

The maintenance stage of change is an ongoing, possibly everlasting, process of sustaining the adjustments you have made. The change isn't new anymore; it's become part of your everyday life. Maintenance can be made easier if you fully accept the change within your identity: seeing it as part of who you are instead of something that you *just do*. You can support this maintenance by creating an encouraging environment, keeping up with skills that are relevant to your change, and by celebrating your progress at each milestone.

In theory, you could stay in the maintenance stage for the rest of your life. If you decided to take multivitamins every day with your breakfast, sure, you could technically keep that up forever. The maintenance phase doesn't mean you've reached a stable, perfect state. Instead, it's usually a period of equilibrium that allows for both growth and the occasional misstep. You've likely gained some new skills and felt the sweetness of your accomplishment. Take note of who you have become and check in with that alter-ego that we created in the contemplation phase.

Is there any more work that needs to be done? Perhaps. Maybe with this new confidence, you see it's time to start the change process all over again in another area of your self-discovery journey.

But you might also need to prepare yourself for relapse.

Relapse

After some time you might have neglected that new mattress, and are noticing that the fabric is tearing at one of the seams. Perhaps it's stained a bit from that spilled morning coffee, and is lumping in areas you didn't expect. Or maybe you're just tired of constantly doing quality control checks on the mattress after owning it for a while. Can all this be repaired, or do we have to replace it once again?

Welcome to the relapse stage, sometimes referred to as the burnout stage, in which motivation is lacking to keep up the progress or something has set us back a step or two.

Relapse is a natural part of the change cycle. Frankly, I think we all should prepare for the relapse phases that are ahead. We often think of change like the flick of a switch—first it's not there, then all of the sudden it's there for good. Change is actually more of a back-and-forth pattern than a linear model.

I want to really emphasize to you that relapse is not a failure; it's a normal and sometimes inevitable part of change. But anticipating a setback can help reduce the shame of it. If you're more prepared for a bump in the road, you'll be able to better recognize that bump as a point of slowing down within your journey instead of a full-stop. View these moments as learning opportunities that help you refine your process moving forward.

Most importantly, practice self-compassion. This message is one that I remind my clients of daily. Maybe it's the high-pressure environment that most of us are operating in these days, but kindness to ourselves seems to be a waning habit. It's okay to hold yourself to a high standard, but make sure to give yourself grace if you don't quite meet the bar that you've set.

If—or more likely *when*—you find yourself sliding backward in progress, there are strategies available that can help you regain your footing and get things back on track. The first is to take a pause. Fair warning here: this might feel a little unnatural. Our instincts during setbacks tend to fall into one of two camps: completely abandon ship because we have failed, or keep pushing through and work harder and hopefully we'll get back into the swing of things. Both of these options completely breeze past learning opportunities. Taking a breather to fully be in the moment can help you pick up on the clues that led to the setback.

Once you've gained that vital information, you can make an informed decision on how to move forward. Perhaps part of the strategy needs to be adjusted to regain forward momentum, or maybe shifting the motivation behind the change can help you realign toward your actions. As you regain your footing, test out your theories with small steps to aid in building back up your confidence.

As you keep going on your path towards change, stay both committed and flexible. Each step, stumble, and recovery are part of the process that will lead to your evolution as a person. Relapse can help contribute to your net growth if you utilize it correctly. When you reach the milestones you were aiming for, success will taste so much sweeter knowing the challenges you were able to overcome to get there.

EXERCISE 4.3 CHANGE REFLECTION

Think of a time you tried to make a change but slipped back into old patterns.

What change was I trying to make?

What led to the setback?
- Lack of support
- Too ambitious/fast
- Lost motivation
- Unexpected stress

What did I learn about myself?

If I tried this change again, what would I do differently?

One strength I showed, even during the setback:

Your Ongoing Journey

I used the mattress example as we went through this chapter to show what one singular change process might look like. In reality, we are touching each one of these stages for different changes at any given time. We might be smack in the middle of the action stage with setting up a fitness routine at the same time that we're in precontemplation about looking for a new job and relapsing with our reading goals.

In reading through this chapter, what bubbled to the surface of your mind in reflecting on the various stages? It might be worth putting pen to paper and charting what stage you're in for different areas of your life.

EXERCISE 4.4 CHANGE STAGES

For each area below, identify which stage of change you're currently in.

Physical Health (exercise, diet, sleep)
- Current stage
- One action step

Mental Health (stress, coping, therapy)
- Current stage
- One action step

Relationships (communication, boundaries)
- Current stage
- One action step

Work/Career (job satisfaction, skills)
- Current stage
- One action step

Personal Growth (habits, hobbies, learning)
- Current stage
- One action step

Living Situation (home, organization, environment)
- Current stage
- One action step

From what you listed out above, reflect on the following.

Which area feels most ready for change now?

Which area am I most resistant to changing?

Based on this assessment, my focus should be:

Assessing Our Willingness for Change

The next section of the book takes a peek into specific lifestyle factors that may influence us in each stage of change. As we move forward, hold onto the knowledge and strategies that you've gained in learning about the Stages of Change model. Let it be a guide in reflecting on your readiness to address the following areas of your life, helping you better understand where you are now and what kinds of changes you are willing to make.

We're about to get more specific and into the nitty gritty. Although this sounds daunting, I find it to be exciting. There's a world of possibilities waiting for you! You're going to be able to apply the Stages of Change model to create more specific and actionable steps within key areas of your life in order to support your mental health and overall well-being.

Chapter 5

Psychosomatic Connection

Your mind and body are like two skilled dancers engaged in a constant tango. They move in synchronicity, alternating between leading and following. This dance is complex but looks effortless, and is the essence of the psychosomatic connection. Our health and well-being are constantly shaped by an interplay between our thoughts, feelings, and bodily sensations, and even our actions and decisions can be guided by the psychosomatic connection. In this chapter, we'll look more closely at the relationship between mind and body issues, and how to help them dance in partnership together.

Psychosomatic means that an emotion is coming up as a physical feeling. And if you're one who's heard it before, the term might come along with either positive or negative connotations in your mind. You would not be alone if that were the case. There are two separate schools of thought that have caught popularity over the past few decades regarding the psychosomatic connection, and they are wildly different.

The first approach originates from practitioners in the medical field who strongly believe that many medical symptoms are made up either consciously or subconsciously by the patient. As a result, patients who are experiencing real symptoms are written off under the assumption that they're "making it up" or "it's all in their head." Or you might know a friend or family member who thinks the idea of feelings showing up as physical aches and pains is a bunch of hullabaloo.

Opponents of this viewpoint argue that, made up or not, any symptoms that negatively impact a patient's life should still be addressed and given the benefit of the doubt. Dr. Peter Attia, author of *Outlive: The Science & Art of Longevity* (Attia & Gifford, 2023), for example suggests the lack of treatment of alleged psychosomatic illnesses is a negligent practice within the currently popular Medicine 2.0 model—in which the field of medicine treats patients reactively rather than through prevention approaches. Attia's proposed Medicine 3.0 model conversely takes a deeper look into causes of medical illnesses and advocates for thorough preventative medical practices. If fully adopted, not only would his Medicine 3.0 approach promote physical health, but it would likely reduce the likelihood of developing psychosomatic and mental illnesses. (Now if only insurance companies could get on board with preventative services!)

Unlike the doctors of Medicine 2.0, I'm in the camp of people who believe that psychosomatic symptoms should be looked at more closely when it comes to physical health. As I said earlier, the dance between mind and body can be led by either dance partner. Getting a headache or sore shoulders after a hard day at work, for example, can be a psychosomatic symptom. Stress zits can follow us from high school into adulthood. I remembered being surprised when someone told me that their sadness shows up in their knees. Almost anything is possible when it comes to psychosomatic symptoms!

Even though this mind-body connection sounds like a new pop-psychology phenomenon, the study of psychosomatics can actually be traced back to Hippocrates. Remember that guy from history class? Much of his medical practice—and the work of many ancient Greek, Persian, and Middle Eastern physicians after him—was dedicated to understanding the link between mental health symptoms and bodily diseases. Even the terminology originates from the Greek language—with *psyche* meaning "soul" and *soma* meaning "body."

Many treatments prescribed by Hippocrates addressed the former: the soul. He believed that you can promote healing in the brain through breathing practices, gymnastics, and praying. Even music was prescribed to treat both mental and physical diseases. Around the same time, Aristotle's approach to medicine influenced the phrase, "a healthy mind in a healthy body," and emphasized the importance of exercise for harmony between the mind and body. Imagine going to the doctor for mental tension from dealing with gout and being told you need to stretch while listening to alternating harp and flute music as a holistic treatment. Believe it or not, this was a real prescription in ancient Greece!

Healing traditions like Chinese medicine and Ayurveda have also long recognized the concept of mind-body unity. Western medicine, however, has sailed away from holistic practices in order to support neat and tidy compartmentalized medicinal practices. (Once again, I find myself blaming insurance companies.) Today, research from neuroscientists, immunologists, geneticists, and psychologists are bringing back the relevance of holistic medical and mental health treatments. They're providing research that supports the idea that our bodies are in an active and reciprocal relationship with our minds.

Psychosomatics for the Everyday Person

When I'm meeting with a new client, I always try to check in on their physical symptoms as well as their mental ones. I ask clients to consider if any symptoms might be related to a medical issue. As many new therapists are often reminded, you can't talk your way out of a solely physical medical illness. There are many symptoms that—while they are easily explained as mental health—are actually signals of a bodily health matter. Experiencing depression, fatigue, and anxiety can come hand-in-hand with conditions ranging from a simple vitamin deficiency to a more complex diagnosis of cancer.

Checking in with your primary care physician can help discover any possible medical root cause of emotional or psychological challenges you are facing. Getting a second opinion may also be worth considering, if you aren't getting the help you need when you do raise the issue. Although functional medicine doctors who consider the whole patient can cost more than traditional healthcare providers who look at clinical symptoms only, I've seen a lot of success for my clients who worked with the former.

Functional medicine doctors, for example, may be more expensive because they typically run more elaborate blood tests to get a full picture of elements that are impacting your physical—and sometimes mental—health. To illustrate: I had one client who was making great progress in therapy to challenge anxious and depressive thought patterns, but whose mood and outlook on life changed even more for the better after their functional medicine doctor pinpointed and treated a hidden mineral deficiency and suboptimal thyroid functioning.

After medical causes are ruled out, we can move forward with better understanding how your mind may be impacting your body. (By the way, *rule out* is another term often used by therapists to discuss cases or document treatment plans and demonstrate that various other factors or diagnoses were considered but dismissed for one reason or another. It's like striking out the name of someone on the suspect list to help the lead detective's thinking process on the case.)

Understanding how both the mind and the body work together in a complex interplay is what we'll focus on next.

EXERCISE 5.1 MY PHYSICAL SYMPTOMS

Check off any physical symptoms you've experienced.
- Headaches
- Stomach issues
- Muscle tension
- Fatigue
- Sleep problems
- Changes in appetite

When did these symptoms start?

What was happening in your life when they started?

Have you discussed your symptoms with a doctor or other appropriate professional?
Yes / No / Not yet but planning to

If not, what's holding you back?

The Therapeutic Spiderweb of Thoughts, Feelings, and Emotions

When I get to the psychosomatic part of the assessment phase with a new client, my clinical mind is bringing up this visual:

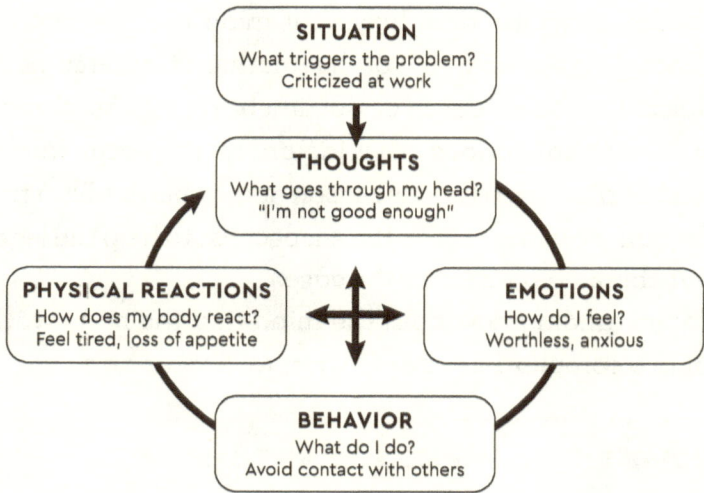

Thoughts, emotions, behaviors, physical sensations, and corresponding situations all interact with one another like ripples in water. A large stone chucked into a serene lake is going to cause quite a stir. Ripples from a change in emotions can collide with the movement of those around behavior, and so on. Each element can manipulate the other—some with larger effects than others. There is no one clear leader of these elements and no chronological order from which one precedes the next: just stones of different sizes tossed in at any time for each category, waiting to be impacted by the others.

Let's consider this common scenario: You're up for an important job interview (situation). You find yourself thinking "Oh gosh, I can't mess this up" (thoughts). As time creeps closer to the start of the interview, anxiety ramps up (emotions) and you start feeling sweaty and immensely aware of your heart trying to beat out of your chest (physical sensations). You might consider ditching the interview altogether in a bout of self-sabotage, or you power through despite feeling a little shaky (behavior).

When we're just starting to notice the connections between each of these elements, it can be difficult to pinpoint the initial catalyst. Was it the catastrophizing thought, the heightened feelings, or the clenched hands that led to each of the other experiences? And once they get going, a spiral can start. For example, your physical sensations can deepen your uncomfortable emotions, which can make your anxious thoughts more fervent. (I would like to formally apologize to all the interviewers who have had to shake my sweaty palms.)

Here's the beauty in this chain of events: if a negative thought or feeling can trigger a downward spiral, a positive one can turn things around. By understanding the interconnection between each of these processes, you can stop yourself from getting caught in the problematic spiral cycle, and you can start to take control with the part that is easiest for you to reach.

If you've got a solid hold on your thought processes for example, replacing an ineffective thought with an effective one might be the trick to try. Or, checking in with your feelings and observing them from a distance might give you space to steer the ship of emotions in a different direction if that's an easier starting place. If physical cues are most immediate, decreasing uncomfortable sensations through breathing or stretching could provide enough relief to address the other symptoms. Simply choosing to engage in a safe and sensible behavior can also be another way to pave the way to emotional regulation.

Paying attention is one of the most helpful steps you can make. Take notice of little signs like when your shoulders tense or when your teeth start to grind. Even take note of what's happening when excited energy floods your body. These are messengers signaling you to be clued into the hidden dialogue between your body and mind. As you start to manage psychosomatic symptoms throughout your daily life, you may become more prepared to work towards resolving larger emotions and physical responses to prevent chronic conditions.

EXERCISE 5.2 PHYSICAL STRESS CHECK

Think of a recent stressful situation. Track how it moved through the different elements.

The situation:
My thoughts were:
My emotions were:
Physical sensations I noticed:
  • Tense shoulders/neck/jaw
  • Stomach knots
  • Racing heart
  • Shallow breathing
  • Excessive sweating

My behavior was:

Which element is easiest for me to notice first?
  • Thoughts
  • Emotions
  • Physical sensations
  • Behaviors

Which element feels most in my control to change?

Long-term Impacts on Physical Health

I sometimes wonder how ancient physicians would react to the data that shows correlations between long-held emotions like anger or sadness and chronic diseases. Although it's hard for people to believe these studies today, I think Hippocrates and Aristotle would respond with an unsurprised, "Duh!"

Modern researchers have found that emotions can impact our bodies beyond just physical sensations or intestinal function (hello, nervous digestion), but all the way down to our cells and our genetic makeup. When you chronically experience stress or intense emotions, it impacts your body in the same way that keeping your parked car's engine on at full throttle would; something is bound to break down. The constant activation of our body's response systems can lead to things like:

- A disrupted hormone balance

- Digestive issues

- Unhealthy sleep patterns which lead to more issues

- A compromised immune system

- Cellular aging and DNA expression alteration

Dr. Gabor Maté has spent much of his career understanding this very concept. He explains in his book, *When the Body Says No*—along with many of his presentations and other written works—that our bodies can act like pressure cookers (Maté, 2003). If we don't find a healthy way to release the building emotional steam, the pressure will find another way to escape. Over his years of work, he has noticed patterns such as women with breast cancer having a history of repressed anger, or the presence of a higher risk of developing multiple sclerosis in grieving parents. Experiencing prolonged bouts of negative emotions, in particular, have proven to be correlated with worsened physical health and higher rates of disease.

But living in denial can lead to a similar fate. Maintaining a false motto of "everything is fine" can still result in a physical toll as the subconscious processes the emotions that your conscious mind is not ready to face. So if feeling our emotions too intensely and for too long can be just as damaging as ignoring them, what are we meant to do? The key is to strike a balance, which admittedly—just like most of the self-help or therapeutic work we have to do—can be easier said than done.

Caring for our emotional well-being is just one piece of the puzzle to improving overall wellness. And, the physical messages we receive from our bodies should be acknowledged as part of that whole. As you've read through this chapter so far, what stood out to you? Tune in to any consistent aches or pains you experience, or pay attention to any health patterns that may arise. Notice if there are any emotions that you're feeling on a more frequent basis, or if there's anything you're actively avoiding feeling. And bring up both to your family doctor and (future) therapist.

EXERCISE 5.3 FREQUENT EMOTIONS

Feel free to reference Exercise 1.1 from Chapter 1.

How do I typically handle difficult emotions?
- Talk about them
- Keep them to myself
- Get them out through exercise
- Distract myself
- Journal
- Avoid thinking about them

Where do I feel these emotions in my body?

Chronic physical issues I have:

Possible connections I notice:

One small change I could try this week:
- Notice my body signals more
- Take breaks when I need them
- Try deep breathing
- Talk to someone
- Move my body

The Connection Between Mind and Body

The ancient physicians were on to something when they recognized that the mind and body are partners in an intricate dance. What we're learning now is just how deep this connection goes—our thoughts and emotions don't just influence how we feel physically, they can impact us all the way down to our cellular structure and genetic expression. I don't want you to leave this chapter having added another layer of anxiety to your life ("Now I feel stressed about my stress making me sick!"), but rather having cultivated empowerment through knowledge that can guide your wellness decisions.

The beauty of the psychosomatic connection is that it works in both ways. Just as persistent negative emotions can create physical symptoms, intentional positive changes—whether through addressing your thoughts, processing your emotions, moving your body, or changing your behaviors—can create an upward wave of improved well-being. When you're able to notice the early warning signals your body sends you, you're building awareness of your internal communication system that can help prevent minor stressors from growing into major health issues.

Remember that honoring the mind-body connection doesn't mean that you need to become hypervigilant to catch every ache or pain, nor does it give permission to dismiss the need for appropriate medical care. (Please go to the doctor when you need to!) Instead, it's about developing a more holistic awareness of yourself. As you move forward, consider how you might incorporate this understanding into your daily life: perhaps you could set a mid-day reminder on weekdays to check in with your body between meetings, create a tracking sheet to note down physical sensations and reflect on possible correlated emotions, or simply give yourself permission to treat both your mental and physical needs as equally important parts of your overall health. As your awareness of the mind-body system grows, you'll be able to get better at working with it rather than against it.

Chapter 6
Sleep Hygiene

As we explored in the previous chapter, the mind and the body are continuously influencing one another. This connection is even more starkly evident when we examine the realm of sleep. When our conscious minds drift off to sleep, it becomes prime time for the body and brain to go through a repair and restoration process. You may have noticed that a bad night's sleep usually results in a cranky mood the next day, just as feeling stressed or troubled during the day can knock your sleep off-balance.

Picture your mind as a movie theater. When you're awake, the movie is rolling while thoughts, emotions, and actions come alive on screen. After the movie fades out and you fall asleep, the metaphorical movie theater crew sweeps up the forgotten popcorn, repairs any damage to the theater or screen, and gets set up for the next showing. If the theater were to push through without this vital break, the quality of the theater would start to diminish.

That's exactly what's happening for over one-third of American adults who, according to a CDC study analyzing data on American sleep, are unable to consistently engage in adequate sleep practices (Liu et al., 2014). I would propose that inadequate sleep affects closer to two-thirds of the population, at least based on those individuals who seek the help of therapists.

There are two main patterns I've noticed between my clients who are experiencing troubled sleep. The first of which is that sleep is less of a priority for those who are hooked on (or trapped within) society's prioritization of capital productivity.

Sleep deprivation is often worn as a badge of honor these days as we collectively value hustle culture and meeting work goals. The narrative of a good night's rest no longer has as much value as the notion of "not wasting time" and squeezing the most out of each day, despite how detrimental it can be to our minds and bodies.

Add in the fact that, for many Americans, navigating the rising costs of *literally everything* in the United States, sleep has shifted from being an easy activity to engage in to a privilege. More people are having to sacrifice sleep in order to meet the bare minimum for survival, and others are putting in long work hours in the hopes of securing a financial future. But the mental health consequences of sleep deprivation in these individuals is equally—if not more so—dire.

The second pattern that's prominent within my client population—and one that I admittedly find myself often stuck in as well—is that sleep is commonly delayed due to content consumption. We live in the beautiful and complex age of information that brings many gifts as well as challenges to navigate.

Back in the caveman days, any morsel of information from our environment or community could have been vital for survival. As a result, our brains are still wired to be a sponge for external information. But now we have access to a mind-boggling surplus of this informational stimuli, which our minds are not equipped for.

Each person has their own tolerance level for data consumption, but ultimately everyone reaches their healthy limit. Even though we're primed to be curious about the unknown, we need to be mindful of how much time we're spending in consuming content. Overconsumption is a quick pathway to mental fatigue that impacts our ability to focus, can often lower our self-esteem, and takes time away from activities and connections that are more likely to support our well-being.

The amount of time spent on screens is another important consideration when it comes to content consumption. Blue light and screen exposure have been the latest culprit in preventing us from getting that quality one-on-one time with our beds for sleep. We'll touch on this more as I'll walk you through *sleep hygiene*, which is the clinical term for routines and practices that impact sleep quality.

Fortunately, sleep remains a well-studied topic within research fields. (This is where we get the benefit of the information age and having access to research study outcomes!) One of my favorite sleep scientists to refer to is Matthew Walker, PhD. In a 2019 TED Talk, he describes the current wave of collective sleep deficit as "the greatest public health challenge we face in the 21st century" (Walker, 2019). It's hard to argue with this claim when a volume of other research studies also continue to link poor sleep to both mental and physical health.

What all of this research points to is that, simply put, if we're not sleeping, we're not recovering. We need that crucial time to let our bodies process the stress from yesterday and to restore balance for today. In my clinical practice, I've witnessed how focusing on improving sleep quality alone can lead to a cascade of improved cognitive functioning, mood, and ability to emotionally regulate.

In order to help you achieve this, next we'll walk through the common experiences that I assess with clients, and then I'll propose an ideal sleep routine that can be customized to your preferences.

What Do I Do with Clients?

Because sleep is so critical to mental health, I like to assess new clients' sleep habits and quality within our first two sessions. I am also perhaps a bit of a "sleep freak," a term I used to call my mother to tease about her over prioritization of getting a good night's sleep, but have since adopted myself. Sleeping through a burglary is a real possibility in my household, since all the ear plugs, eye masks, and white noise machines would make the job a real cake walk. But the impact good sleep has on our family's well-being and overall happiness is more valuable than anything someone might steal. So it's safe to say that I hope to help everyone reach an improved state of sleep.

During assessments, I tend to do a fire round of questioning with clients regarding their sleep habits. The main areas I'm looking at are: typical sleep duration, rest quality, circadian rhythm, chronotype, and overall routine (or lack thereof). Let's break each of these down.

Sleep Duration

Although it varies person to person, the ever-famous bench-mark of getting eight hours of sleep is generally still a great guideline to follow. The National Sleep Foundation (2020) rec-ommends the following durations based on your age:

- Teenagers (14-17 years): 8-10 hours
- Young adults (18-25 years): 7-9 hours
- Adults (26-64 years): 7-9 hours
- Older adults (65+ years): 7-8 hours

But healthy sleep isn't just about hitting a specific number of hours; we also need to take the sleep cycle into account. Humans take 90 to 110 minutes to complete one quality sleep cycle, which includes one stage of rapid eye movement (REM) sleep and three stages of Non-REM sleep. These Non-REM stages are when the body is in repair-mode, while REM sleep involves the mind creating dreams, processing emotions, and moving memories from short-term storage into long-term stor-age. The optimal amount of four to six total sleep cycles is rec-ommended per night. (Think: the movie theater is completely clean and ready for another film.)

If you're cognizant of timing your sleep cycles, then you're more likely to wake up feeling refreshed. Interrupting your sleep in the middle of a sleep cycle can make it difficult to get out of bed or can contribute to grogginess throughout the day. So, when planning out your bedtime and morning alarms, these cycles are important to consider. In addition to aiming for a minimum of, let's say, seven hours of sleep each night, try to reach the optimal amount of four to six total sleep cycles.

Don't worry, there's no need to bust out a calculator before bed; there are plenty of apps available to help with figuring out ideal sleep or wake times before you get settled into a routine.

Need to take a nap during the day? The recommended sleep times again can vary by individual, but research suggests a 10- to 20-minute power nap is ideal for a pick-me-up in terms of performance and alertness. If you need more than that, aim for the full 90-minute REM cycle. Anywhere in between might catch you smack dab in the middle of a sleep cycle, and cause you to feel more tired post-nap than you were before the snooze.

EXERCISE 6.1 SLEEP TRACKING

Track your sleep for a week (estimate if you can't remember).

For each day of the week note the following.
- Bedtime:
- Wake time:
- Hours slept:
- Quality of sleep (1 to 5):
- How you felt the next day:

What patterns did you notice from tracking?

Rest Quality

When it comes to REM, the quality of your sleep cycle is crucial for a good night's sleep. Just as fast food impacts our bodies differently than "home cooked" meals made with natural ingredients, we want to focus on the quality that will better serve us for the long-term. The "home-cooked meal" of sleep would entail falling asleep easily, sleeping solidly throughout the night, hitting the deep and REM stages of sleep, feeling rested and alert upon waking, and being able to repeat this pattern consistently.

Though this is ideal, it can understandably be tricky to achieve these days. Using screens before sleeping can cause overstimulation that requires extra wind-down recovery time, in addition to blue light disrupting melatonin production in your body. Caffeine and nicotine can also contribute to difficulty in falling asleep, while alcohol consumption can interrupt sleep quality after you've already started to sleep.

A sedentary lifestyle or uncomfortable physical conditions, like restless legs, heartburn, or chronic pain, are other barriers to good quality sleep. Medications to treat physical conditions might cause issues, too. Prescriptions for anxiety, depression, and blood pressure are particularly known for impacting sleep patterns. Then there are also mental health considerations for sleep. Stress and anxiety can keep your mind in overdrive, making sleep difficult to achieve.

These factors all contribute to getting the "fast food" version of sleep. Sure, you may have met the basic requirements needed by your body, but at a cost of overall quality. Frequent waking or shallow sleep prevent you from feeling rested, and inconsistent sleep patterns can create a sleep deficit (or even a sleep surplus) that is stored in your body and impacts future sleep quality.

Most of us are engaging in multiple lifestyle choices that can bring us joy but negatively impact sleep quality. I'm not suggesting to completely cut off your coffee habit, screen time routines, or change your job simply for the sake of being well rested. Instead, I'd recommend making small tweaks to your routine, one at a time, to slowly reach improved sleep quality over time. As we discussed in previous chapters, slow and steady wins the race.

Circadian Rhythm

The circadian rhythm is an umbrella that covers all the technicalities that lead to our specific sleep and wake patterns, and ultimately, our chronotype. It operates on a twenty-four-hour cycle, influencing hormone production, core body temperature, and metabolism—biological processes that are largely reactive to light exposure. Sunlight and bright light signals your body that it's time to be awake, and gives you a jolt of cortisol to help you get up, just as the absence of light tells your body that it's time to produce melatonin and call it a day.

Our bodies tend to release insulin more throughout the day rather than the night, similar to how the average metabolic rate is higher during day time as well. This means that glucose utilization, nutrient processing, and energy storage are all more efficiently done during daylight hours. Your typical core body temperature pattern also has a peak temperature in the afternoon, when most people are active, then dips in temperature as the day leads to night. A lower and stable body temperature at night helps the body repair and promotes restful sleep. So any disturbances in thermoregulation can take a toll on your circadian rhythm and therefore overall sleep quality.

The biggest takeaway when it comes to considering your circadian rhythm is to follow your body's natural cues and patterns. If you're able to, avoid the "social jet lag" that comes with working across different time zones, or extending your day unnecessarily with an abundance of artificial blue light. Break up the monotony of the indoor lifestyle and get exposure to natural sunlight in the morning and the night sky at the end of the day. When your biological and social clocks are working together, you're more likely to have improved sleep.

Chronotype

If you're having a difficult time identifying your typical circadian rhythm patterns, it may be worth identifying your specific *chronotype*. Chronotypes and circadian rhythm are interlinked, with chronotype being a label for the subtype of circadian rhythm pattern that people tend to fall into. Each one of us has an individual chronotype variation. The main categories are:

Early Birds (Morning Chronotype). These individuals are naturally early risers and prefer to go to bed on the early side rather than staying up late. When it comes to being productive, getting a head start at the top of the day works best for them.

Night Owls (Evening Chronotype). Their biological clocks lean towards a later sleep and rise time. Peak performance for night owls tends to be later in the day, and sometimes even quite late at night before finally hitting the hay.

Hummingbirds (Intermediate Chronotype). Falling somewhere in between the morning and evening chronotypes, people who resonate with the intermediate category have a flexible schedule and can adapt well to scheduling demands. They feel reasonably alert throughout the day, with best productivity times varying from person to person.

Although many of us identify ourselves off the bat as an Early Bird or Night Owl, the intermediate chronotype is actually the most common. Genetics, age, and external factors like societal or cultural norms can all impact your chronotype. Working a regular night shift at the hospital or committing to early morning rowing team workouts can lead you to adapting to a more optimal chronotype for your schedule. That said, your chronotype can, and probably will, shift throughout your lifespan. Younger folks tend to live a Night Owl lifestyle easily, then move towards Early Bird preferences as they age.

There is no right or wrong chronotype, but it's important to try to work with your body's natural rhythms. Fighting your chronotype can be like trying to swim upstream. I learned this lesson recently, as I tried to get myself to set aside writing time for this book at 5 a.m. While such an early morning alarm was a breeze in my early twenties, I realize that is no longer the case. In facing reality, I have accepted my current Night Owl routine (despite it not being my preference) and usually find my writing stride around 11 p.m.

You can plan your day more optimally when working around your chronotype, saving easy tasks for when you're less motivated and doing more demanding activities at the times where you have the most energy. You can build on your chronotype knowledge by incorporating things that align with your natural circadian rhythm to prevent any disruptions in your typical sleep pattern.

EXERCISE 6.2 BUILD YOUR CHRONOTYPE

Curious about your chronotype?

When do you naturally feel most alert and energetic? (Select one)
- Early morning (6am to 9am)
- Mid-morning (9am to 12pm)
- Afternoon (12pm to 4pm)
- Evening (4pm to 8pm)
- Late night (8pm and later)

If you had no schedule restrictions, when would you naturally go to bed?

When would you naturally wake up?

When do you do your best work/thinking?

What would you guess your chronotype is?
- Early bird
- Hummingbird
- Night owl

How well does your schedule match your chronotype?
- Very well
- Somewhat well
- Not well at all

What's one thing you could change to better honor your chronotype?

Sleep Routine

This is the part of the assessment phase when I ask clients about their bedtime routine, and to really get into the nitty gritty with each and every detail. After determining what their current habits are, I encourage my clients to amend them in order to follow the practical strategies laid out by Heather Darwall-Smith, a psychotherapist and sleep specialist in the United Kingdom, in her book *The Science of Sleep* (2021). I've created a bedtime checklist using her advice and observations from my own clinical practice is as follows:

- Establish a consistent bedtime schedule: going to bed and waking up around the same time each day helps regulate your internal body clock.

- Create a relaxing pre-sleep ritual: it can be as short as five minutes, but engaging in the same wind-down activities every day before sleeping helps clue your brain into knowing it's time to sleep.

- Set your room up to optimize sleeping conditions: keep your room as dark as possible, use earplugs or noise machines to block out noise disturbances, and keep the room temperature a little below 70 degrees to support your body's sleep needs.

- Regulate your light exposure: get out in the daylight while the sun is out and minimize screen exposure at least an hour prior to bedtime.

- Be mindful of your food and drink consumption: avoid large meals before bedtime that can cause physical discomfort or heartburn, as well as overconsumption of caffeine or alcohol which can disturb sleep quality.

- Exercise during the day: while physical activity can have an energizing effect if done just before bedtime, a regular daytime exercise routine promotes better sleep.

- Manage stress: engaging in meditation or journaling can help clear your mind so you don't get stuck in a mental spiral while you lay in bed at night.

Practice self-compassion when working through this checklist. Reviewing all these practices can be overwhelming at first, and sometimes there are unavoidable barriers that can keep us from implementing them. Having control of your room temperature, ability to create a consistent bedtime schedule, engaging in physical exercise, or having control over meals can all depend on life circumstances, and in many instances may be a privilege difficult to obtain.

If you find that there are restrictions in your life impairing your ability to implement any of these checklist items, be kind to yourself and move on to the ones that you are able to control. These elements are building blocks to better sleep, not rigid rules to follow. When conditions shift, you can change your bedtime practices accordingly.

EXERCISE 6.3 CURRENT SLEEP HABITS

Rate your current habits. (1 = never, 5 = always)
- Consistent bedtime:
- Consistent wake time:
- Relaxing pre-sleep ritual:
- Cool, dark, quiet room:
- Limited screens before bed:
- Mindful of food/drink type and timing:
- Regular daytime exercise:
- Manage evening stress:

Identify your biggest sleep disruptors.
- Screen time
- Caffeine or alcohol
- Stress and/or racing thoughts
- Uncomfortable room
- Irregular schedule
- Late meals
- No wind-down routine

List three changes to try this week to help your sleep.

Brainstorm your ideal bedtime routine.
- 2 hours before bed:
- 1 hour before bed:
- 30 minutes before bed:
- Right before bed:

Sleep as a Foundation for Mental and Physical Wellness

Remember when I compared your sleep cycle to a movie theater? I want to conclude this chapter by emphasizing that you are the manager of the movie theater, in charge of the ongoing screenings and theater cleanings over time. There will be crises and technicalities to manage, but the theater ultimately benefits from an intentional manager.

Good sleep is more than just a reset button from the day, it's a precursor to good mental and physical health. We process emotions during deep sleep, consolidate memories, and allow both our brain and body to recover and prepare for the next day. Over time with better sleep, you'll likely notice improved stability in your mood, less brain fog, more emotional resilience, and better stress management.

Remember that quality of sleep can also fluctuate in waves as we experience changes throughout life. Great sleep is less of a destination and more of a journey. School, work deadlines, parenthood, and general life adversity can knock you off-kilter. Be mindful of the aspects of sleep that you do have control over at the moment and focus on those.

Sometimes you can set up everything to be in your favor and still have bad sleep. If you experience this, you might benefit from calling in the experts. Medical conditions, medications, and sleep disorders can be examined and treated by medical professionals and sleep specialists. Sleep tracking apps and online tools are a great resource to utilize to gather data for the experts, or to aid any changes you're wanting to implement with your sleep routine.

The clients I have worked with who modified their sleep for the better have seen a surge of positive effects throughout the rest of their day. Although it takes work and intentionality to improve sleep, the benefits can start showing up even as soon as you take the first step of change. Caring for your sleep means that you are caring for yourself. Sweet dreams!

EXERCISE 6.4 SLEEP GOALS

What are your sleep goals for the next month?
- Consistent 7 to 9 hours nightly
- Better sleep quality
- Earlier bedtime
- Less screen time before bed
- Better energy in the morning

How will you track your progress?
- Sleep journal
- Phone app
- Simple rating scale

What support might you need?
- Talk to a doctor
- Sleep study
- Change of sleep environment
- Help with stress management

If you don't see improvements by this time next month, you will:

Chapter 7

Nutrition

While sleep provides a nightly reset for the brain and body, the meals we eat supply the essential fuel for recovery and basic functioning throughout all of our systems—keeping both our bodies and our minds running at optimal levels. So in this chapter, we will focus on another important vertebrae in the backbone of mental health: nutrition.

In general, I try to assess a new client's eating habits within the first two sessions if possible, because not only is everyone's relationship with food a little bit different (and can therefore tell me a bit more about who they are and what their life is like), but the nutrition we gain (or miss) from the types of food we eat can have an impact on mental health. It is a great lifestyle area to focus on near the beginning of therapy, as identifying small changes that might be made in eating habits can yield mental health benefits, but doing so also pinpoints any potential need for further specialized support.

Before I jump into the different areas of food and eating to assess, however, I want to acknowledge something important: a person's relationship with food can be complex. It's meshed with culture, lifestyle, emotions, economics, and relationships. If food is a particularly sensitive topic for you right now, I invite you to move ahead to the next chapter if you need to. We will not be specifically discussing eating disorders in this chapter, but I recognize that many of the following topics may be stressful to engage with if you are struggling in your relationship with food. I also want to highlight that none of the following topics or areas of assessment are meant to be shaming. Instead, they're meant to be considered without judgment. Nutrition awareness isn't about creating rigid rules or eating perfectly, but gathering information to find a balance that's right for you.

Core Assessment Areas for Nutrition

Meal Patterns and Timing

The basics of a client's eating habits are the first thing I like to gauge when it comes to conducting food assessments. This includes frequency, timing, and common patterns. To understand the baseline relationship that new clients may have with food, I like to ask questions like: Do you eat when you're hungry or when your schedule allows meal breaks? Does your level of hunger or lack thereof impact your mood? Do you notice how your typical eating patterns feel in your mind and body in any positive or negative way?

I'm not here to police what your meal or snack frequency looks like, or how much you're eating overall. The truth is, we all have different needs based on our genetics, metabolism, medical concerns, and lifestyle. Over the past decade or so, pop culture and lifestyle media have cycled between recommending small and frequent meals or larger, spaced-out meals. Until the unlikely event that scientists find the ultimate eating plan that works for every human on the planet, my advice is to truly listen to your body and your mood, and give yourself what you need most, when you need it. But doing so may require some attention and intentionality.

For example, over time, I've learned that I'm a snacker. In the morning, sometimes I'll go for a protein shake, oatmeal, or my favorite chocolatey cereal, and I tend to end my day with a solid meal too—but all that time between breakfast and dinner? That's snack time! I get bored with repetitive meals and stressed out about the ambiguous expectations of what lunch should entail. Instead of adding another meal to the day, whenever I'm hungry I'll nibble some cheese, maybe a little bit of leftovers from the prior day's dinner, or anything else that grabs my attention that day.

While snacking can be a little mindless at times, full meals on the other hand naturally tend to require a mindful—or at least intentional—setting, simply due to the increased effort to both cook (or acquire) and eat them. So if snacking isn't your jam, you may find this approach to be more beneficial for you and your mental wellness. For example, although he's not totally anti-snack, my husband gravitates towards the full-meals-only side of the pendulum when it comes to his eating. A consistent breakfast, lunch, and dinner routine helps him feel grounded and organized throughout the day. Like him, you may find that having to plan or prepare for meals is a form of self-care that may otherwise be missed.

Before moving on to types of food that can impact mental

health, we should touch on other routine-based nutritional practices like intermittent fasting or time-restricted eating. These are eating patterns that have become more widely practiced over the past several years, for reasons varying from religious to metabolic. For individuals who can implement them easily and without any negative emotional repercussions, I think these approaches can be great. There is a risk of harm, however, for people who feel stress around scheduled fasting or pressure to engage in restrictive eating patterns. I would advise you to first check with your doctor before taking on these approaches to eating, and then monitor your thoughts and emotions as you try out a new eating pattern.

EXERCISE 7.1 EATING HABITS

Note your typical eating schedule.
Breakfast: Time? Food Eaten?
Lunch: Time? Food Eaten?
Dinner: Time? Food Eaten?

You notice that you tend to eat when:
- You're physically hungry
- Your schedule allows
- You're bored
- You're stressed
- It's "mealtime"
- Food is available
- Emotions are high

How does hunger impact your mood?
- Hanger is real
- You don't notice much difference
- You get anxious when hungry
- You lose focus when hungry

Your eating pattern feels:
- Chaotic
- Somewhat structured
- Very structured
- Just right
- Needs work

One small change you'd like to try is:

Nutritional Impact on Mental Health

Before we look into the *types* of foods being consumed, I want to reiterate that this section is not meant to shame or patrol your diet. That would be outside the scope of my role as a therapist and, quite frankly, a bit rude. On top of that, there are ever-increasing barriers to accessing the types of foods and meals that are most beneficial for mental health. A young single mom whose budget is primarily focused on paying the rent is going to have a different meal plan than an older, married person who is on sabbatical. Time and money are two important resources that are waning for the general public but critical for eating in a way to support mental health.

As we start to cover foods that may impact mental health, please remember that this information is not meant to suggest that you should never eat these foods, or even feel bad about eating them. Restrictive eating and added shame around eating is likely to worsen mental health more than consuming any particular thing. Instead, I simply want to walk through the following findings to arm you with knowledge. You know yourself better than anybody, so you are the best judge on how to implement balance and change to match the unique needs of your body.

When it comes to nutrition and foods for optimal mental health, I often like to refer to the work of Dr. Uma Naidoo when discussing their impact. As a Harvard-trained psychiatrist and trained nutrition specialist, and author of *This Is Your Brain on Food* (2020) and *Calm Your Mind with Food* (2023), Dr. Naidoo is one of the leading experts in the up-and-coming nutritional psychiatry field. The main point she drives home throughout her impressive body of work is this: avoid inflammatory foods in order to protect mental health, because chronically inflamed gut results in an inflamed brain and nervous system.

What's considered inflammatory?

- Foods and drinks with added or refined sugars (like my childhood favorites, Nutter Butters and Kool Aid)

- Processed foods and meats (sausages, deli meats, or frozen meals)

- Stimulant drinks like coffee and alcohol

- Industrial vegetable oils (highly processed oils that lose their nutritional value in processing, unlike cold-pressed oils)

- Gluten (most commonly found in bread and wheat products, but can be sneakily found in places like soy sauce and toothpaste)

Collective groan, I know. That sounds like most of my favorite things! But even though everyone has different tolerance levels for each of these, overconsumption of any can result in at least being bogged down for the day, or perhaps even worsened mental health until the inflammation that results in your gut can calm down.

As someone with a highly active sweet tooth and weekly purchaser of takeout pepperoni pizza, this was a tough pill to swallow. Do sweet treats and meals that make our hearts happy need to be abandoned for good? As it turns out, not necessarily! The key is to avoid a *chronically* inflamed gut. Although in theory it would be ideal to eradicate these inflammatory foods from your diet altogether, circumventing this aspect of gut health can be an unrealistic task for many in today's society. Focusing instead on bringing things in balance can be much more achievable for the average person.

If you want to add to your diet rather than substract, foods known for reducing inflammation and boosting brain health—according to Dr. Naidoo and backed by research—are whole foods. The promotion of healthy gut bacteria and anti-inflammatory ingredients in these foods creates a great launching pad for a healthy brain, and therefore, improved mental health. We're talking about:

- Unprocessed nuts, seeds, and legumes
- High-fiber veggies and fruits
- Prebiotic and probiotic foods (most high-fiber foods will cover your prebiotics, while probiotics are found in fermented foods like kimchi or foods with live cultures like yogurt and kefir)
- Foods with monounsaturated and polyunsaturated fats (again, think whole foods like eggs, avocados, fish, and cold-pressed oils)

If you have an inkling that your mood might benefit from a shift in eating, I recommend listing out everything you've eaten over the past few days or week. Highlight any foods that might be causing you issues. Then consider whether you need to pair another food with what you've been eating to balance out your nutritional intake, like adding a protein to a meal of simple carbohydrates, or if you should try out a food swap. (I've recently tried swapping out chips for carrots. While that was not the most sustainable switch, as I ditched the carrots after a few days, I found that switching from canola oil to cold-pressed olive oil has been a pretty easy replacement!)

Keeping a simple food log over a few days may provide helpful or even surprising insights. I don't recommend rigidly monitoring your food intake if you find heightened focus around eating to be distressing—but if you want to casually check in with your eating patterns and find possible correlations to your moods and emotions, then here's an easy template to try out.

EXERCISE 7.2 WEEKLY FOOD LOG

Fill this in for every day this week.
- Day:
- Foods Eaten:
- Moods & Emotions:

Is there any addition to your typical eating patterns you might be able to make to support your mental health better?

Ideas you could try include:
- More fiber-rich foods
- Probiotic foods
- Healthy fats
- More whole foods
- Better hydration

For the purposes of this book, we're just dipping our toes in the pool of nutritional psychiatry. I've simplified some of the main points from leading experts in the field to help with building awareness around your meals and how you feel, but there are lots of other resources available if you wish to explore this area of your health further.

Mindful Eating and Drinking

Another great starter skill that can help you make the most of meal and snack times is mindful eating. Have you ever sat down to watch a movie with your popcorn and you suddenly hit the bottom of the bowl, hardly realizing you polished off the entire serving? This sounds like my typical experience at the movie theater, finishing my snacks mindlessly before the trailers even end.

Mindful eating switches from zoned-out munching to tuned-in eating. We're wanting to be mentally present and in the moment when consuming foods or drinks, not only for the physical benefits like more effective digestion, but also for managing emotional eating, fine-tuning your mind-body connection, and increasing your overall enjoyment of each meal. For example, I routinely wrote this book with an iced matcha latte in front of me. I resisted the urge to drink the whole thing in one go before the ice cubes melt, which is my typical battle. Instead, I started with small sips. I noticed the bitter flavor of the matcha, then the sweeter taste after I added a drizzle of simple syrup. I listened to the sound of the ice clacking as I stirred my drink, and I noticed the texture—how whole milk is creamier than my usual oat milk order.

Staring at the last remaining sips of the now-diluted drink,

I can tell that being mindful while consuming it was more pleasurable than my go-to chugging method. I had more dopamine-inducing moments as I tuned in to my drink over an extended amount of time. I also feel more physically comfortable, which I can say is not the same experience when I quickly consume pretty much anything. When I happen to give into a faster pace of eating or drinking, a stomach ache and bloating are sure to follow, along with a more irritable mood.

Do I take my own advice and practice mindfulness every time I sit down for a meal? No, and I don't think that's possible for most people. Choosing one meal, snack, or beverage during which you practice mindful consumption to start with will get you into the habit more successfully rather than trying to be mindful every single time. Give it a try if you have a morning coffee (or matcha), a typical afternoon snack, or a regular time to sit down for dinner. Once you're able to consistently practice mindful eating or drinking on a consistent basis, it'll be easier to expand in other areas of your life.

EXERCISE 7.3 MINDFUL EATING PRACTICE

Choose one daily eating/drinking moment to practice mindfulness:
- Morning coffee/tea
- Breakfast
- Lunch
- Daytime snack
- Dinner
- Dessert

For your chosen moment, practice noticing:

Taste. What flavors do you notice? Sweet, salty, bitter?

Texture. Smooth, crunchy, creamy, chewy?
Temperature. Hot, cold, room temperature?
Sounds. What do you hear while eating/drinking?
Pace. How quickly are you consuming this?
Physical sensations. How does your body feel before, during, and after?

After practicing mindful eating/drinking, did you:
- Feel more satisfied
- Enjoy the experience more
- Eat/drink a different amount than usual
- Feel calmer or more relaxed
- Notice things you haven't before

Finding Good Alternatives When They Work for You

Again, there's no absolute right or absolute wrong when it comes to when, how, and what you are eating. What matters is how you feel when and after you eat. If convenience foods are lowering your energy and decreasing your ability to focus, it might be worth considering whole food-swap options. Perhaps finding an alternative food would be a good choice if your favorite macaroni and cheese is causing havoc on your digestive system and making you physically—and then emotionally—uncomfortable.

Maybe you've found that preparing a whole breakfast early in the morning is cutting in on your personal reflection time, and therefore a handful of trail mix is all you need to get the day started, until you can take a break for a more mindful late-morning meal. When it comes to the types of foods you're eating, mindfully considering what you have access to, how it meets your unique needs, and whether it keeps you feeling good is the best in my book.

EXERCISE 7.4 NUTRITION GOALS

Based on this chapter, you might say your top nutrition priority is:
- More consistent meal timings
- Better or different food choices
- Mindful eating practices
- Reducing inflammatory foods
- Adding brain-healthy foods

One specific, small step you'll take this week:

Potential barriers you might face:

How you'll practice self-compassion if you struggle:

You will try to avoid judging yourself for:

What your definition of "good enough" nutrition for your current life situation is:

Chapter 8
Physical Activity

As we wade into the final chapter focusing on the link between our bodies and brains, what stands out to you so far? Is there anything you're excited to try, or have you noticed some resistance in challenging a habit or two that could use tweaking? The first reaction many of my clients have is to roll their eyes or even feel a little annoyed to hear again and again about the benefits of diet, sleep, and exercise. Trust me, I'm familiar with this frustration—we already see advice for improving any of these areas of our lives all over magazines, blogs, and video platforms. The reason I'm bringing these lifestyle considerations to your attention is that, for better or for worse, they *really do* make a difference.

Fortunately, you do not need to conduct a whole overhaul of your life, in the ways we so often see touted on social media. There are going to be times (likely more often than not) when perfect sleep, eating practices, and physical activity will just drop off the radar. All three of these areas have been shaky at times in my own life. Not so long ago, my sleep quality was impacted by having to work at night as I lived abroad, with poor-quality sleep once I finally hit the hay, since my son decided to be nocturnal from birth. My diet consists of more greasy, but delicious, takeout than I would logically prefer, and my exercise is spotty when doing home workouts are the only choice.

The point is not to be perfect at everything or to shame ourselves when we're falling short of the goals we've set. I hope instead to arm you with knowledge that you can keep in your back pocket until the time is right to implement the changes that feel right to you. Personally, I plan on getting a gym membership or trying out a pilates studio and seeing if changes in eating habits will follow. So as you reflect back on the past few chapters and move forward through the next, notice what seems doable, what might be saved for later, and where you can practice some self-compassion in approaching these topics.

The Science of Movement and Mental Health

Our Chemical Factory

From ancient health advice to modern research studies, exercise is well-established as a reliable way to decrease stress and boost your mood. Similar to sleep and nutrition, exercise can influence many of your brain and body's neurobiological functions. Moving your body can result in an increase of those classic "feel-good" neurotransmitters: dopamine and serotonin. Exercise also releases endorphins, which are the hormones known to reduce stress, alleviate pain, and stabilize mood. Cortisol, our occasionally pesty stress hormone, typically decreases after physical activity, too. (Keep the names of these hormones in mind, we're going to get more scientific in this section!)

Experts like Dr. John Ratey also recognize that exercise supports brain growth and plasticity, calling physical activity the "Miracle-Gro for the brain" (2008). This is due to the increased levels of brain-derived neurotrophic factor (BDNF) our muscles produce when we exercise. More BDNF in our systems means better memory recall, cognitive functioning, and ability to learn.

On paper, this math adds up rather well, right? Move your body to increase the production of positive hormones while also modulating the potentially harmful ones. But sometimes that is a *lot* easier said than done. Many of us struggle with mental blocks that make the seemingly simple idea of moving around a bit more feel like a gargantuan task. If you had P.E. class in a middle school like mine, maybe you associate the locker room to be full of judgmental mean girls and the gym environment to be crowded with arrogant jocks. Perhaps the barrier is rooted in body image, whether you're hesitant to do an activity that will make you more aware of a body you are uncomfortable in or if you're nervous about potential changes to your physique.

But what if we didn't have to start off with big changes for your lifestyle or body? Literally any form of movement—even just in small bursts of time, like a quick dance break in the kitchen—can boost your nervous system and aid your mood. If you're chasing that "runner's high" by going all-out with extensive marathon training, then more power to you! But low-stress workouts like walking, and mobility or impact-conscious exercise practices like yoga or swimming, can yield the same net positive effects. Pretty much any form of movement can nudge your brain and body's chemical factory to a healthier and happier production line. Let's look more deeply into how.

Physical Benefits

When our bodies feel better, our minds feel better. Exercise not only provides direct hormonal benefits to our brains, but helps improve other areas of our lives that can impact our moods, too. For example, sleep quality generally improves when physical activity is added into your routine. While vigorous exercise right before bed might actually be overly stimulating and make it harder to fall asleep at bedtime, the hormone and body temperature changes from working out earlier in the day has been shown to regulate our bodies' natural circadian rhythm (Shen et al. 2023).

Lowered cortisol levels plus the release of endorphins that come from exercise also combat a common obstacle for falling asleep: stress and anxiety. Exercise helps calm your mind and enhance your mood, helping you get out of your head and ready to sleep. The increased production of serotonin during exercise also helps with sleep, as serotonin is the precursor to our main sleep hormone, melatonin. Not only do these chemical reactions help us feel better during the day, but they help us sleep better at night—something we discussed at length in Chapter Six.

When we are awake, regular exercise also helps regulate our energy levels. Intentional physical activity engages your cardiovascular system, which helps your heart pump oxygen and nutrients to the cells throughout your body, refreshing and reinvigorating them. When you participate in regular exercise over time, insulin resistance can also improve, blood sugar levels can stabilize, and energy crashes can be prevented (Bor-hade et al., 2025). On top of that, our metabolism and mito-chondrial function become more effective when we're consis-tently physically active, which supports the energy demands of our brains for focus, emotional regulation, and general brain functioning.

The last physical benefit I'll touch on is that exercise helps reduce inflammation in our bodies. Inflammation is a natural response in our blood and body fluids that often signals that there's something wrong, whether there's a condition that's caused by the inflammation itself, or if the inflammation is a resulting symptom of an injury or illness. Chronic inflammation that goes untreated impairs metabolism, damages neural net-works and neurotransmitter production, decreases immunity, and increases fatigue and brain fog (Hötting & Röder, 2013). But physical activity targets the proteins associated with in-flammation and increases the circulation of immune cells, which helps your body repair and recover (Ignácio et al., 2019).

When we exercise, we promote our immunity, protect our energy, and enhance our sleep. Each of these facets of our lives can have a great impact on our mental well-being. Think back to the last time you woke up from a good night of sleep, or when you were finally able to breathe through your nose after recover-ing from a nasty cold. Didn't you feel so much better than when you were tired or sick? Incorporating exercise into your routine aids in all these aspects, keeping you feeling better physically, which helps you stay feeling good mentally.

EXERCISE 8.1 MOVEMENT & MOOD ASSESSMENT

How often do I currently move my body intentionally?

- Daily
- 3-4 times per week
- 1-2 times per week
- Rarely
- Never

Types of movement I currently do:

- Walking
- Gym workouts
- Sports
- Yoga or stretching
- Dancing
- Household activities

When I do move my body, I notice:

- Better mood
- More energy
- Better sleep
- Less stress
- Clearer thinking
- More confidence
- No real difference

My biggest barriers to exercise are:

- Time
- Energy
- Money
- Self-consciousness
- Past negative experiences
- Physical limitations

One small movement I could add to my day:

Symptom-Specific Benefits

Beyond boosting overall brain health, current research shows that exercise can be a direct treatment for certain mental health symptoms (Smith & Merwin, 2021). The same systems that create and regulate the hormones and neurotransmitters that are produced or moderated by exercise (dopamine, serotonin, endorphins, and cortisol) are regulated and targeted by many *psychotropic medications*—a.k.a. the medications prescribed for mental health symptoms. While medication is a topic to discuss with your medical provider, you may be able to alleviate some of these mental health symptoms through exercise:

- **Depression:** dopamine and serotonin are the most common neurotransmitters addressed by antidepressants, which are naturally released during exercise. Endorphins, which are less commonly prescribed for depression due to the addictive nature of the medications (opioids, for example, which act similarly to endorphins), are also naturally produced with exercise and can address depression. (Stanton et al., 2014)

- **Anxiety:** Physical tension in the body can be released through exercise, helping provide relief of *somatic* (a.k.a. physical) symptoms. The most common category of medications prescribed for anxiety reduction are those that help your brain produce or absorb more serotonin, but the serotonin production and cortisol reduction from exercise can also help mitigate feelings of anxiety. (Kandola & Stubbs, 2020)

- **ADHD:** An increase of dopamine and norepinephrine—whether elevated through the metabolization of medications or the natural exercise-associated release from the body—helps with sharpening focus and aiding executive function in individuals managing ADHD symptoms. (Vysniauske et al., 2020)

- **PTSD:** Trauma impacts the nervous system, and conditions such as post-traumatic stress disorder often come with additional depression or anxiety symptoms. While the hormones and neurotransmitters associated with exercise tackle these additional symptoms, exercise itself also helps individuals with trauma heal their nervous systems by reducing hyperarousal. (Hegberg et al., 2019)

- **Bipolar:** In addition to managing the depressive symptoms that come with the downward swings of being bipolar, exercise can help individuals cope with hypomanic symptoms, too. Be aware however, that exercise can worsen manic symptoms for some, so a tailored exercise routine you devise with the guidance of medical or psychiatric specialists is recommended. (Lafer et al., 2023)

By helping with your general brain health and cognitive ability, exercise can also aid in preventing or delaying cognitive decline and diseases like Alzheimer's. But you should always check in with your doctor about treatment of any of these symptoms, as they can walk you through medication options or give you a green light for exercise that targets symptom reduction.

EXERCISE 8.2 EXERCISE AS A TARGETED TOOL

Symptoms I experience:
- Depression/low mood
- Anxiety/worry
- ADHD/trouble focusing
- Stress/overwhelm
- Low energy
- Sleep problems
- Mood swings
- Physical tension

For my most challenging symptom, which movement might help?

I most need a boost:
- In the morning
- During the afternoon slump
- Times of high stress
- More anxious than usual

Exercise as an Intervention

Maybe you don't currently align with a specific mental health diagnosis, but you would still like to feel more mentally healthy. There are many ways to use exercise as a tool for a better you, from using it as a way to regulate our emotions to creating a social network. I like to playfully refer to these as "hacks," but truthfully, using exercise as an intervention usually requires some consistency. So while I don't have many one-time miracle life-improving injections when it comes to exercise, some tweaks to your routine might yield great mental health results.

Mental Mechanisms

The most one-off and as-needed way to inject exercise into your life is when you need a distraction. Maybe you need to take your mind off your worries, that upcoming project deadline, or as a getaway from your best friend's (or your own) Eeyore-like malaise. Engaging in exercise—whose base function as a catalyst for change—can help with providing a temporary distraction, if not even a larger redirection.

On a larger scale, engaging in physical activity means switching up your environment (perhaps weight lifting at the gym or surfing in the ocean). Even if you stay in the same place, like doing a home workout next to the couch you've been planted on all day, you still experience physical changes. And even the most minor change creates a shift in your energy that helps create a break from a previous mindset. Paired with focus that sharpens while exercising, you've got the perfect recipe for a temporary distraction.

If you stick with the same few methods of exercise, you'll likely also find satisfaction in gaining mastery over the specific skills you use. The more often you visit the rock climbing gym, the easier you'll be able to navigate the various routes. Or perhaps you'll find that you can knock a few more seconds off your mile-running time when you hit the treadmill a few days a week. Even if "mastery" feels like too lofty a goal, the small improvements made over time will still grant a sense of achievement that can improve self-esteem.

Dedication to movement can also result in the opportunity to consistently reconnect with your body and deepen your sense of bodily awareness. (Like Mindful Eating, discussed in Chapter 7.) As you engage in regular movement, you'll start to notice subtle shifts in your posture, physical tension, balance, and breath. You might realize your shoulders could be rolled back during your meetings in the boardroom, or that the stressful moment at home could be alleviated slightly by relaxing your muscles and breathing more deeply. This heightened awareness not only helps to understand your body's unique signals and needs, but it can also boost your confidence, grace, and intentionality in the way you move through the world.

Another unexpected, positive side-effect of exercise is that you can gain new social connections through your preferred type of physical activity. Pickleball, for example, has been sweeping the nation not only because it's a fun new sport to try, but because it's created a whole new social scene where people can create teams, compete in leagues, and play with friends in their free time. CrossFit gyms have also been known to create a community feel, and pilates studios might have you finding that the same few interesting people tend to join the same classes you do. Creating a social network—which also boosts your mental health—through exercise not only helps to maintain a consistent routine of physical activity, but also have fun while doing it.

Targeted Exercise

Therapists often have a collection of specific types of exercise in their back pocket that help target various emotions or somatic symptoms. My second therapist, the one after my initial experience which was a flop, recommended yoga to help with my anxiety symptoms. While I wasn't a fan of yoga at the time, I find myself years later booking a class whenever my chest feels too tight from anxiety. The intentional breathing and the fluid movement almost always take my anxiety down a notch or two.

In this way, exercise can be a great crisis management tool. It's important to have realistic expectations, though. Many of my clients hope that the exercises I suggest will completely dissolve their unwanted symptoms. While this is rarely the case, the right exercises should be able to "take the edge off" and help you get back on your feet to some degree. If you stick to the same exercises and practice them even when you feel grounded and emotionally regulated, it should be more effective when you try the exercises as an intervention in a more turbulent moment.

One of my favorite ways to use exercise in treatment is with couples. You would not believe how effective it can be to break the tension when couples take a jumping-jack break in the middle of an argument. The change of activity and alteration of brain chemicals generally help the couple switch gears in their discussion. As the couple notices how their heartbeats and body temperatures return back to normal after the jumping-jacks, each partner also tends to be more grounded and calm when moving back into the conversation.

Slower-paced exercises for those of us who need to quiet our minds and calm our bodies can work just as well. I've had multiple clients claim that a stretching routine at the start of their day helped in supporting a grounded and stable morning, and even quiet their mind to relax before bed. Calisthenics, pilates, and simple, gentle movement can help set the tone for the day by encouraging a flow state of mind that is paired with intentional psychosomatic connection.

Finding Your Match

If you've already got a good workout plan going, then keep it up! But most of us bounce between phases of being active and phases where we just can't be bothered to get moving. If you want to tap into your body's feel-good chemical factory for the extra benefits, finding the right type of exercise could support your ability to add consistent physical activity to your routine.

When it comes to finding the right exercise approach, let's return to the idea from Chapter Two of experimenting. We often feel a lot of pressure around the topic of exercise because it's so heavily associated with sentiments of self-esteem and body image—on top of all the emphasis I've put here on how good it is for your mental health! But try as best you can to set aside any fear of failure. By experimenting with exercise, we're just gathering data to find the right fit for you.

Of course, please consult with your doctor if you have any relevant health concerns that limit you from any particular type of activity.

EXERCISE 8.3 EXERCISE EXPERIMENT PLANNING

Activities I've enjoyed in the past:

Activities I've disliked:

What made them enjoyable or unenjoyable:

Exercise experiments:
- Activity:
- When/Where:
- Cost:
- Timeline:

What I'll track when experimenting:
(Choose two to three to test over the next month)

Success criteria:
(What would make an exercise worth continuing?)

Using Physical Activity for Personal Growth

Although my intention with this chapter is to make exercise sound approachable and universally beneficial, I know that it can be a complicated topic for many. Mandatory participation in school P.E. programs might have left a negative mark on some (raising my hand), resulting in an avoidance of exercise for years or even decades, while others are still physically and mentally recovering from a sports injury or long-term illness. If deciding to get up and work out was as simple as it sounds, we would all be wildly fit, both in body and mind.

I hope that this chapter has helped you gain at least one degree of curiosity in how the right physical activity might complement your life and your mental health goals. The minimal positive outcome of exercise could be some neurotransmitters and hormones that transition a bad day into at least an okay one. Or you might find a whole new community that turns your world upside-down for the better.

EXERCISE 8.4 MOVEMENT GOALS & SELF-COMPASSION

My realistic movement goal for the next month:
- Move my body for 10 minutes, three times a week
- Try two new activities
- Walk more during daily activities
- Do morning stretches
- Find one activity I actually enjoy

How I'll remember to be gentle with myself:

If I "fail" at my goal, I will:
- Adjust the goals appropriately
- Try a different approach

- Remember that small progress still counts
- Practice self-compassion

My motivation for moving more:
- Better mental health
- More energy
- Stress relief
- Social connection
- Sense of accomplishment

Support I might need:
- Workout buddy
- Professional guidance
- Equipment/access
- Childcare
- Schedule adjustment

Chapter 9
Social Support

Have you ever been to a big college football game or watched sports fans celebrate a victory together? There's something positively contagious about the excitement and shared joy, from high fives with strangers to collective cheers and chants. Not a fan of football? Luckily sports and fitness communities aren't the only ones waiting for you to join and share the fun.

If you're like me, you may have a tendency to view previously established friend groups and communities as exclusive clubs with bright neon "No Vacancy" signs directed at us. Many of us often convince ourselves that the social circles others around us are enjoying are airtight, with a full roster of members and no room to budge. Looking into the mirror, however, has there ever been a time when you and *your* friends actively rejected a potential new group member? The chances are that you've historically been more open to new connections than not.

The truth is that most friend groups and communities are

more akin to a cozy cafe than an exclusive club. Sure, there are regular members who have established close connections with the baristas, but there are also open tables and seats available to newcomers. Each individual adds their own unique layer to the cafe ambiance.

In this chapter, we'll start to understand why social connections are so important for our mental health and well-being, and how to engage with them. We'll check out the different types of communities available to us—from book clubs to community volunteering groups—to see which ones might give you that same sense of belonging as the cheering sports fans seem to find together. We'll also address any of the barriers that are holding you back from reaching out and getting involved.

At the end of the day, we're all humans looking for meaningful connections. As we go through this chapter, whether you're starting from scratch or wanting to deepen your connection in existing groups, remember that there's always room for one more person at the social table.

Why We Need Social Support

Have you ever had someone bring you hot soup when you were sick, or a friend respond to a panicked late-night text with the perfect meme? Beyond being just nice gestures, these are examples of social support in action. In a society that keeps leaning towards a "me, myself, and I" focus, simple connections like these can reduce stress, improve our coping mechanisms, give us a sense of belonging, reduce the risk of mental illness and bolster our resilience.

For the purposes of this chapter, I want to propose four types of social support. As we go through these variants, keep in mind that you might not relate to each one, and that's okay. We want to start with bolstering at least one of these areas, and then expand into the others. As you might know by now, I'm a big fan of starting small! Slow and steady wins the race.

Types of Social Support

The first type of social support, and the one that quickly comes to my mind as a therapist, is the **emotional support** that we hope to receive from others. Emotional support from someone looks like a friend listening to you vent when you need to complain about your noisy neighbors or giving you a warm hug of congratulations right after getting some good news. Personally, I really value being able to have go-to people who are willing to give me a hug or say "that sucks" when I'm going through something difficult. Or conversely, having my own personal cheer squad to support my "wins" in life and celebrate with me. Receiving emotional support means that you're getting the empathy, reassurance, and caring words or actions that validate your feelings. Being seen, heard, valued, and understood helps us regain confidence and feel secure throughout life's ups and downs.

The people we most often gain emotional support from are the friends and family members present in our lives. They know our struggles as well as our strengths. However, you can also tap into professional resources for emotional support. Seeing a therapist or joining a support group can fill a gap in emotional support that might be missing in your current connections.

Instrumental support, unlike other types, offers tangible, tactical assistance for any needs you might have when it comes to living your life in a smooth and healthy manner. This might be having a go-to person or service to help with laundry and groceries, or assistance in walking through financial concerns like establishing a household budget or filing your taxes. This is your A-team in getting things done!

For many of us, life can start to get complicated as we become independent adults. Parents, guardians, and school systems act as our first line of instrumental support, but as we graduate from schools and leave the family home to start our own adventures, we end up having to rely on ourselves for daily tasks and practical needs. When those things start to become overwhelming, tapping into friend networks or professional services can provide much-needed relief.

Speaking of schools and thinking about workplaces—these are key environments to lean on for *informational support*, a critical element when it comes to guiding your big decisions. Teachers, professors, and advisors provide knowledge that shape our educational journeys. Mentors, supervisors, and co-workers can similarly guide our professional growth.

But informational support is not limited to these environments. Having a friend or mentor to advise about leasing a car versus buying one can be crucial in guiding your decision-making process. Your acquaintance who just bought a house might be able to give you insight on the home-buying process, just as your healthcare's Diabetes Support Group can help you understand how to navigate your new diagnosis.

Appraisal support, which is almost a blend of emotional support and informational support, is unique in that its goal is to help you grow. Think of appraisal support like coaching. Someone giving you appraisal support might be providing you with constructive feedback on your presentation at work, or new songs to try when practicing your musical skills with the trombone. They'll help you evaluate your present circumstance and attain new skills or confidence to move forward.

An example from my own life is my childhood tennis teacher, whom my friends and I affectionately referred to as TTD (Tennis Teacher Dude). In our weekly lessons, TTD always let me know when my volley was strong or how my backhand could be a little less wobbly. Although I'm no Venus or Serena Williams, I grew comfortable playing tennis thanks to his appraisal support.

As you may have noticed, one individual can provide several different types of support. Family often serves as our first experience of each type, with friends and teachers stepping up to the plate next. Not everyone is privileged to receive each type of support from immediate connections, though, and that's when seeking outside support can be useful. If you're willing to try them out, professional services, clubs, tutors, and other networks can be accessed to reach support that isn't organically available in your life.

The Stress-Buffering Hypothesis

One of the strongest cases for the importance of social support in mental health stems from the stress-buffering hypothesis, which was originally introduced by researchers Sheldon Cohen and Thomas Ashby Wills in 1985. This hypothesis proposes that having social support can act as a protective barrier for your mental health, like an umbrella that keeps you dry in a storm of stressors.

Being on the receiving end of social support doesn't just feel good—it actually changes how our brains and bodies respond to distressing stimuli. Could an interaction with the right friend or family member make me feel better after I opened my credit card statement? The answer is yes! This is because the *mirror neurons* in our brains (the ones that make us yawn when we see someone else yawning) are particularly sensitive to direct interactions with others. When we talk about mirror neurons in terms of emotions, regulating our own by mirroring someone else's is known as *coregulation*. So if you're with a friend who is feeling calm, you'll start to feel more calm, too.

Even more meaningful? After you've spent time with your support people or communities, the positive effects continue to carry over. Coregulation results in more oxytocin (the relaxing "love hormone"), less cortisol (remember that stress hormone?), and even lowered blood pressure (Bornstein & Esposito, 2023). It's as if our bodies were designed to chill out and recover when we're around the right people.

When we receive the physiological benefits and comfort that come from one of the four types of social support, our shields against life's challenges are fortified. The stress-buffering hypothesis has the potential to cause positive ripples throughout the rest of your day and help you overcome anything from addiction to stage fright.

Assessing Your Current Social Network

Before starting a new social scene from scratch, let's take stock of the existing connections in your life. Examining your support network like you might your pantry, which items in there are fresh and nourishing, and which ones might be in need of a healthy swap? I've created the below exercise to help with mapping your current social support to see what's going well and what might need improving.

EXERCISE 9.1 SOCIAL SUPPORT INVENTORY

People who provide me with Emotional Support:
(listening, empathy, celebrating with me)

People who provide me with Instrumental Support:
(practical help, favors, tangible assistance)

People who provide me with Informational Support:
(advice, guidance, sharing knowledge)

People who provide me with Appraisal Support:
(feedback, coaching, helping growth)

Rate your satisfaction with each type:
(1 through 5, with 5 being very satisfied)
- Emotional support:
- Instrumental support:
- Informational support:
- Appraisal support:
- Which type of support do you need more of?
- Which relationships feel most balanced?

Building & Engaging with Support Systems

Building

Now that you have a sense of what's working for you and what isn't in terms of your social connections, let's imagine that you've just moved to a new town and the only familiar person you're able to find is the one in the mirror. (You!) Creating all-new social connections can be daunting, but the optimist in me finds some excitement in it, too. While it's all too easy to be swept up in our everyday interactions, it's not often that we feel like we can take a step back and be intentional in the connections we forge, but this is a great opportunity to do so with fresh eyes.

Focusing on small, achievable goals will best bring your vision to reality. From the assessment above, which area would you like to target first? If you noticed a huge gap in your ability to receive appraisal support, then seeking a coach or mentor might be a good first step. Or if you have close friendship ties but weak family relationships, you might want to start by checking in with the family members you'd like to strengthen your bond with.

Wherever you want to begin, think of yourself now as the architect in building your new ideal social network. It's much easier to construct something out once we have the blueprints, and basing those plans off your imagined dreams is a great place to start. Incorporating your passions and preferences will also make establishing your social support network that much more motivating and satisfying.

Consider your natural social style to help guide your plans. If you're an extrovert, you may imagine daily lunch outings with coworkers or being able to host regular dinner parties with new friends. Perhaps volunteering every weekend with a local non-profit could comfortably be added to your calendar. Maybe you're an introvert who would be much more comfortable with one-on-one meetups every once in a while, even wanting to find friends who are free for quick text convos instead of consistently meeting in-person.

If you are someone who wants to build social connections around your existing passions or hobbies, then established networks like pottery classes, skills workshops, and improv groups provide a reliable environment to connect with others who share similar interests with you. Are you into more niche topics like maximalist interior design? Check out online groups where you can meet like-minded souls and form online friendships or launch an in-person friendship.

Another question to consider logistically: what is a realistic timeline for making new connections? While for some it may be amazing to skyrocket to the most popular person in town by next week (which is not impossible in this age of people going "viral" online), it's more common to experience a slow build when it comes to forming community. Realistic timeline practices could include prioritizing at least one in-person coffee meeting a week, DM'ing friends from the past to reconnect with each month, or trying out new community groups each season as the weather changes. You can go as fast or as slow as you'd like, following your intuition and figuring out what rhythm makes sense for you.

As you plan to widen your social support matrix, check to see if there are any obstacles that you should also prepare for. We all have impactful interactions from the past that still haunt us to this day, for example: that brutal rejection from your high school crush or the disappointment when a seemingly close friend faded away. Even though we can intellectually write these interactions off as one-time experiences, the emotional scars can linger and emerge as fear when approaching the possibility of forging new relationships. Other common barriers include having a "too busy" schedule with little wiggle room for socializing, geographical constraints for meeting up with new people, and the little voice in the back of your head telling you that there's nobody new out there for you to connect with.

Take note of the hurdles that are likely to pop up throughout your social efforts. It may be worth making a written plan to prepare for them in advance. The process of making and growing connections is a continuous process, so whether you feel stuck or discouraged in one week or in one year, having an action plan to refer to can provide clarity throughout the journey.

EXERCISE 9.2 SOCIAL NETWORK BUILDING PLAN

My social style:
- Prefer one-on-one interactions
- Enjoy group settings
- Like planned activities
- Prefer spontaneous hangouts
- Online connections work for me
- Need in-person interactions

Areas where I'd like to build connections:
- Hobby/interest groups
- Professional networking
- Neighborhood/community
- Fitness/wellness groups
- Volunteer organizations
- Online communities

Realistic timeline for building connections:
- One new interaction per week
- One new group or activity per month
- Reconnect with one old friend monthly

Potential obstacles I might face:
- Social anxiety
- Time constraints
- Past rejection experiences
- Geographic limitations
- Financial barriers

My action plan to overcome these obstacles:

One specific step I'll take this week:

Engaging

Once you've started building out your network, utilize a mindful approach for consistently engaging with the connections you hope to maintain. By keeping regular windows of time available to connect with others—almost like office hours, but for friendship—you ensure that there's adequate time built into your schedule for prioritizing socialization. And if you feel the need for an introvert retreat creeping up on you? Then great—you can use that blocked off time for self-care instead.

There are many skills for maintaining friendships that, from what I see from my clients in therapy, start to wane as we enter society at large. Too often we get sucked into the daily routine that comes with work or managing kids and other family responsibilities, and as a result social connections get pushed to the back burner. Additionally, because of the COVID pandemic and ensuing quarantine, many young adults experienced a disruption in their critical social skills during formative school years, leaving them underpracticed in developing relationships of all kinds (Juvonen et al., 2022). So if I were to create a blueprint for how to keep connections strong, here's what it would look like:

1. Practice Vulnerability

If you take away anything from this section, I'd hope that it would be to practice healthy vulnerability in relationships. I'll admit, this is a delicate balance. We want to avoid the two extremes here: being so guarded that nobody gets to know the real you, and being such an open book that people who just met you learn your whole life story upfront. The anxiety that underlies both of these extremes comes from wanting to have some degree of control in whether or not others accept you. (Because deep down, we all want to be accepted for who we are and avoid any sense of rejection.)

A healthy middle ground involves intentional and bound-aried conversations with others. As my previous supervisor, Simi Markar, would say when talking with clients about appropriate vulnerability: let others earn the privilege of getting to know you. Be honest in presenting yourself to others, while also letting the process of establishing closeness unfold over time. In a world where it seems everyone is posting their entire lives online, and perfectly curated lives at that, seeing someone show up authentically in everyday, in-person interactions is becoming increasingly special. People are drawn to authenticity—and ultimately the best relationships are the ones within which you can be true to yourself—so don't be afraid to be yourself when connecting to others.

2. Be Curious

Here's a motto that guides my favorite conversational tip: curiosity keeps the connection. (Feel free to turn it into a jingle if that helps you remember it!) Being an active listener who asks questions that express sincere interest can immensely help your efforts to engage in existing relationships. If you had a friend who was constantly on their phone when you met up, or a coworker who spent more time bragging on their success than actively participating with their team, would you put more effort into those relationships? Or would you pivot your attention elsewhere?

My advice: don't be like that "friend" or coworker. Dig a little deeper and ask the detail-oriented questions that easily get skipped when conversations stay on the surface level. Some of my favorite types of questions or statements to deepen conversations actually come from therapeutic techniques, such as:

- Reflective statements—"It sounds like you've been spending a lot of time training for your triathlon."

- Strengths-based statements—"It must have taken a lot of stamina and resilience to train six days a week."

- Open-ended questions—"How did you become interested in doing triathlons?"

- Imaginative questions—"If you could have a superpower to help with any one aspect of the race, what would it be?"

3. Maintain Reciprocity

Relationships often require some level of balance. For example, people tend to not move beyond acquaintanceship into a deeper relationship if one person is clearly more domineering, is always happy to have the other person pay for lunch without ever offering to cover a cost in return, or more frequently waits for the other to initiate meet ups.

One way I like to think about reciprocity is in terms of love languages, pioneered by Gary Chapman in his book *The 5 Love Languages*. These five types of love languages are referred to as: words of affirmation, acts of service, physical touch, quality time, and receiving gifts. Personally, I stink at giving gifts but receiving gifts is a top love language for my best friend. So I always keep my eye out for something that would be meaningful for them, even though gift giving does not come naturally to me. As you work on strengthening your social support network, pay attention to the way others try to initiate interactions with you, because "speaking their language" may help in deepening your connection.

Lastly, consider getting ahead of the connection curve by doing favors for others. As humans, we tend to feel the desire to return niceties that we received. I don't share this tidbit to encourage you to be a master manipulator; rather, I approach generosity as being a win-win habit. Not only do we feel better when we help people out, but we are also more likely to promote future positive interactions with others when we are proactive in coming to their aid.

4. Focus on Repair When Things Go Wrong

Two common themes I've noticed amongst my clients when it comes to any sort of dissolved personal relationship are miscommunication and a lack of repair work. "Ghosting" is not just a phenomenon amongst the dating scene anymore—it's become a norm across all social interactions. There seems to be a mindset shift from unquestioned loyalty (which, admittedly, is not always healthy) towards a "plenty of fish in the sea" attitude throughout both personal and professional relationship priorities. This results in many people choosing to cut and run when things get even remotely challenging (or awkward, or boring, or requiring change), instead of even attempting to strengthen bridges.

Many people, at least in American society, are generally conflict-avoidant and lean towards people-pleasing tendencies, so the desire to shy away from tough conversations is understandable. But no matter how hard we try to avoid friction with others, it's impossible to prevent it entirely. I think the most powerful tool in preserving relationships today is the ability to put our egos to the side and say, "I'm sorry. I messed up." Or, "That didn't go the way I hoped it would. Can we try again?" Like authenticity, being able to appropriately express your point of view while also claiming responsibility for your shortfalls is a valuable skill that helps sustain the support that keeps you—and others—mentally healthy.

EXERCISE 9.3 RELATIONSHIP SKILLS SELF-ASSESSMENT

Rate your current skills.

(1 through 5, where 1 = very strong)

>   **Vulnerability:** (Sharing appropriately and authentically)
>   **Curiosity:** (Asking questions and showing interest)
>   **Reciprocity:** (Giving and receiving in balanced ways)
>   **Repair:** (Addressing conflicts and misunderstandings)

List examples of each skill in recent interactions.

>   **Vulnerability.** When did I last share something meaningful?
>   **Curiosity.** What's a good question I asked recently?
>   **Reciprocity.** How do I typically show care for others?
>   **Repair.** How do I handle conflict or misunderstandings?

>   **What's one skill I would most like to improve?**

>   **What is one way I'll practice this skill this week?**

Digital Age Considerations

Before we move on to the next chapter, I want to highlight some unique considerations that come from utilizing the Internet for social connection. We live in a beautiful, exciting (and sometimes scary) time of having an entire online world to engage with. I remember a Social Psychology class from my undergrad curriculum in which we discussed social patterns of the past as compared to now. As humans, our social lives used to be restricted to only the other individuals physically near us. Oftentimes that meant that people only interacted with others from the same culture, social rules, religion, education opportunities, and geographical resources (such as sharing common locations like the local garden or grocery store, or village healer). For most of human history, actually, societies have consisted of relatively homogenous groups.

Comparatively, we now literally have the whole world available to us at the tap of a finger! We get to learn about other societies, and interact with people who have backgrounds that widely differ from our own. Being able to expand our worldview and create relationships with people whom we otherwise would have never bumped into from our geographical bubble is an amazing gift of the digital age. At the same time, there are aspects of the Internet that can be damaging to social connections and our mental health.

There are two common concerns I have for clients who are frequently engaged in online socializing: comparison and isolation. When we scroll through social media, we're getting hit with a wide spectrum of other people's curated highlight reels. We're taking in a handful, and sometimes even *hundreds*, of other people's achievements, best moments, and thrilling experiences—all while comparing our behind-the-scenes reality either consciously or subconsciously. The constant exposure leads to a "comparison trap" that has us feeling inadequate about our own lives and experiences. Prevent falling into this trap by practicing context awareness. Remind yourself that you're seeing a brief snapshot, and practice boundaries around the amount of time you spend on social media or types of accounts that you follow.

The second common concern that clients come to me with is the (almost ironic) experience of feeling isolated as a response to being on social media. Despite being more "connected" than ever before, many people report feeling lonelier after spending time online. Digital interactions can lack the depth, nuance, and emotional regulation benefits like coregulation that come from face-to-face interactions. Likes, comments, and brief DM exchanges are less fulfilling than in-person connections. Try to instead use social media and digital interactions as a stepping stone to real-world engagement. This could look like joining online sports fan groups with the intention of attending safe in-person games, or staying in touch with long-distance friends online while planning a road trip together to a mutually exciting concert.

I'm not going to suggest ditching the online world to get the benefits of social connections—healthy Internet and social media usage involves being intentional about how and why you engage with others online. To feel satisfied with your quality of social connections, I would instead advocate for using digital platforms to supplement, not substitute, your in-person interactions. Set specific times for checking social media to avoid mindless scrolling, practice appropriate and safe levels of vulnerability for online interactions, and deepen your relationships by focusing on meaningful conversation instead of surface-level emoji exchanges. You can even conduct a periodic "digital audit" to assess whether your online activity is contributing to your sense of connection and well-being, or if it should be adjusted to better support the deeper relationships your mental health truly needs.

EXERCISE 9.4 DIGITAL RELATIONSHIP AUDIT

How many hours do I spend on social media daily?

After social media use, I typically feel:
- Connected
- Informed
- Inspired
- Lonely
- Inadequate
- Anxious
- Envious
- Neutral

Online interactions that feel meaningful to me:

Online interactions that leave me feeling worse:

Changes I could make to improve my digital relationships:
- Limit scrolling time
- Unfollow accounts that trigger comparison or unhealthy emotional reactions
- Use online connections to plan in-person meetings
- Be more intentional about who/which platforms I engage with online
- Share more authentically

One digital boundary I'll set this week:

Building Meaningful Connections

While we've shifted as a society to seeing social support as a nice-to-have in life, it actually plays a critical role in our mental well-being. The stress-buffering effects of meaningful connections, the coregulation that occurs when we're around supportive people, and the practical assistance we can both give and receive all contribute to a more resilient, fulfilling life. Whether you're starting from scratch after moving to a new city or you're hoping to deepen existing relationships, remember that meaningful connections are built gradually through consistent interactions over time.

As you work on expanding your social support network, be patient with yourself and others. While you may not become the best friend of everyone in your town, you certainly set yourself up for success socially by showing up as your authentic self, practicing healthy vulnerability, and engaging with others using genuine curiosity. Try to cultivate a few meaningful connections that provide the emotional, instrumental, informational, and appraisal support that support you to thrive. Most importantly, don't forget that being a good friend to others is just as important as receiving support. The simple act of giving care to others is itself a powerful contributor to your own mental health and sense of purpose.

EXERCISE 9.5 SOCIAL SUPPORT GOALS

My top priority for social connection right now:
- Building one meaningful new friendship
- Deepening existing relationships
- Finding my best-fit community
- Improving family relationships
- Developing professional connections

Success would look like:

Support I might need to achieve this goal:
- Help in identifying where to meet people
- Therapy to work on social anxiety

- Practicing difficult conversations
- Childcare for social activities
- Transportation

How I'll be patient with myself during this process:

Red flags that would signal I need professional help:
- Persistent social anxiety
- Difficulty maintaining relationships
- Feeling isolated
- Excessive fear of social interaction

Chapter 10
All About Boundaries

Our final chapter addressing foundational aspects of mental health continues our focus on the social realm—this time all about boundaries. Establishing and sticking with boundaries are such critical yet complex skills, that most of us have to learn them progressively over time. I'll offer some self-disclosure here: I totally sucked with boundaries until my late twenties. My general lack of boundaries led to me totally overextending myself and getting burned out in jobs, feeling embarrassed when I consistently shared too much in social situations, and holding resentment for others when I went overboard with making commitments. And even when I started learning to create and hold them, my journey with boundaries has continued to be a gradual learning curve.

Does any of this sound familiar? When we don't have the right boundaries in place with others, and even with ourselves, we can end up stressed out and frustrated. Over time, prioritiz-ing others and putting their assumed needs above ours can lead to emotional exhaustion and even loss of our own identity. This results in a disconnect from our intrinsic wants and needs, and can damage our mental health. Conversely, if we're too rigid in implementing unhealthy boundaries, we can end up experienc-ing isolation and damaged relationships.

Healthy boundaries give us balance. They allow us to par-ticipate in an equitable give-and-take dance with others, which helps support mutual respect and connection in relationships. It also prevents resentment. The right boundaries will pro-tect your mental and emotional well-being while allowing you to stay committed to your personal values and needs when it comes to being in relationship with others. When we're able to focus on what matters to us, we can hold on to our self-identity with a higher level of confidence , which ultimately leads to be-ing more loving and generous with others.

What I particularly want to stress throughout this chapter is that the right boundaries are *healthy* ones. The cultural shift in society lately has been promoting what I consider to be un-healthy boundaries. I've been seeing a lot of advice lately that looks like: "Cut off any relationship that drains your energy," or "You don't need to explain your boundary; they need to accept it." While this rigidity may be useful as self-advocacy in toxic relationships, it can do more harm than good in healthy ones.

If there's no urgent need to establish safety and distance with another person, then I would recommend slowly wading into the waters of boundary-setting and being gentle with both yourself and others as you do so. Each person's boundaries are going to look different according to their wants, needs, and values.

As we go through the next few sections, I want to also ac-knowledge that the larger discussion of boundaries tends to come from a Western mindset that prioritizes individualism. If the following few sections don't quite resonate with you and your cultural background, I invite you to hang in there until the last section that addresses other approaches to boundaries.

We will touch on cultural and self-regulation considerations towards the end of this chapter—not because they're not im-portant, but because I want to end our discussion on boundar-ies on a thought-provoking note that helps us zoom out and see a holistic picture of how we can prioritize our mental health in a way that acknowledges outer systems, which will ultimately help in creating more effective boundaries.

Boundaries 101

Oftentimes when I bring up the topic of boundaries in therapy sessions, my clients express a vague understanding of what they are, but confusion around how to implement them in their own lives. The topic feels big and ambiguous, and even scary for those of us who have been living with few boundaries and passive communication styles. Most of my clients respond with something to the effect of "Where the heck do I even start?" Well, first, let's clarify what boundaries are *not*.

A common misconception is that boundaries are personal ground rules that everyone else needs to abide by. Or insisting that others avoid your "triggers" so that you can feel comfort-able. These controlling requests that hide under the disguise of boundaries might sound like, "You're going to make me an-gry if you keep pointing your finger at me when you talk so you better stop before I snap." Or, if I were to choose ones from my own arsenal, "Don't tell me what to do," and "Stop chewing with your mouth open, it makes me want to crawl out of my skin." But alas, relationships tend to do better when we work on controlling *ourselves* and our reactions rather than micromanaging the other person.

Effective and healthy boundaries define what *you* will or won't accept, instead of trying to change someone else's behavior. (I cannot repeat this enough—boundaries are about you, not about controlling others.) Once you get the hang of shifting responsibility from others to yourself, I'm sure you'll be able to really get the boundary-ball going. I'll list out some examples of healthy boundaries later on in this chapter to help you brainstorm what might be needed in your life. To provide some clarity in the meantime, we can use the example of shifting from, "You need to stop texting me when I'm at work," to a healthy boundary of, "I won't be available for messaging when I'm working."

Now that we've dug into the reality of what boundaries are, we can wade into the waters of what it would look like for you to implement and stay consistent with your own boundaries.

Brainstorming Boundaries

So how do you know where you might need a boundary or two? The best indicator is any area of your life where you are feeling drained, uncomfortable, or resentful. Notice if something feels consistently off in certain types of relationships or environments. Maybe you're always overcommitted at work and feeling burned out, or you're tired of never being prioritized by friends in the same way that you value them. You may have guessed it by now—we need to tap into our self-awareness to get insight on where boundaries might support us best.

As you become aware of the situations or patterns that lead to a less-than-ideal feeling, ask yourself, "What do I need to feel valued or respected here?" If this is still too broad of a question for just starting out, it can be helpful to consider instead which type of boundary could be the most useful: physical, mental, emotional, temporal, or material. These can be understood as:

- **Physical.** How you're situated within an environment, your preferences with personal space or touch, or what level of privacy you're comfortable with.

- **Mental.** What type of thoughts you have, the values you respect.

- **Emotional.** The energy level you want to maintain and protect, and the feelings that come up for you in your mind and body.

- **Temporal.** Needs and responsibilities that have a time-based element, including scheduling and personal routines.

- **Material.** The financial resources and physical items that belong to you and are important for you to safeguard.

We can break boundaries down even further under any of these categories into *expressed boundaries*, those that we implement by telling it to another person, or *internal boundaries*, which we hold ourselves to. While an expressed boundary could be "My availability for meeting up with friends is shifting from weeknights to weekends only," a similar internal boundary would sound like, "I will prioritize my self-care on weekdays so that I can be fully present for my friends on weekends."

As you read through these categories and types of boundaries, what areas of your own life came to mind? Are there any relationships, environments, or situations that fall into one or more boundary types? As examples come to you, check back in with the earlier question about what you need in these situations. Perhaps establishing physical distance in professional environments can help you breathe easier, or expressing confidence in your own opinions can help you feel heard in social situations. Let's go through a few more examples before we talk about how to implement and stay consistent with your boundaries.

EXERCISE 10.1 BOUNDARIES ASSESSMENT

List areas where I feel drained, uncomfortable, or resentful.
  At Work:
  With Family:
  With Friends:
  In romantic relationships:
  In social situations:

Answer these questions for each of the above areas identified.

  Type of boundary needed? (physical, mental, emotional, temporal, material)

  What I need to feel valued and respected?

  How urgent is this to address?
  (1 to 10, with 10 being most urgent)

What Healthy Boundaries Look Like

As you read through the following examples, notice the details that sound applicable to the various aspects of your own lived experience. Take what fits in your life, and adjust the ones that might not be totally spot-on for what you need. I've kept the examples in the same five categories, to help narrow down which one is most needed in your life.

Physical

- "It's more comfortable for me to greet people with a wave or verbal hello rather than hugs or handshakes."

- "I need to step outside for some air at times when I'm in a crowded or overwhelming space."

- "I keep my bedroom as a private space but guests are more than welcome to hang out in the common living areas."

Mental

- "I don't engage in conversations that involve gossiping about mutual friends or coworkers. However, I'd love to chat about…"

- "I'm choosing to not talk about politics with my immediate family members to preserve our relationships."

- "While I don't feel comfortable giving advice on major life decisions, I'm happy to listen and support you in your journey of finding the answer that feels best for you."

Emotional

- "I need to take a step back from this conversation when voices are getting raised. We can revisit this topic when we're both feeling more calm."

- "I care about you and I'm concerned that I'm not able to fill the role as your primary emotional support person. I think a counselor could be helpful and I can be a supplementary support person."

- "I'm not able to take responsibility for managing other people's reactions to my decisions."

Temporal

- "I don't check work emails after 7 PM or on weekends so that I can prevent burnout and be fully present when I am on the clock for work responsibilities."

- "I'm not sure that I can commit to social plans that are made last-minute, but I'd still like to receive the invitation in case my schedule allows for me to join."

  "Sunday mornings are reserved for my personal routine, but I'll be available most Sundays by noon for calls or visits."

Material

- "I'm not able to lend out my car right now. If you need help in finding an alternate mode of transportation, I'd love to help with your search."

- "I'm comfortable with contributing $30 for the group gift, but I can't afford to spend much more than that."

- "I prefer to only share my financial information with my spouse, so I'm not able to disclose my salary or expenses."

EXERCISE 10.2 CREATING BOUNDARIES

Using the examples as inspiration, write two to three boundaries that you may find helpful to implement.

Identify the following for each boundary above.

- Is this an internal boundary (something I hold myself to) or an expressed boundary (something I communicate to others)?
- How comfortable do I feel implementing this? (1 to 5, with 5 being most comfortable)
- What's my biggest fear about setting this boundary?

Putting Boundaries in Place and Sticking With Them

Here comes the scary part: putting your boundaries into action. Just like any new skill, don't expect to be perfect at it on your first few attempts. If there's a little voice somewhere in your head saying that setting necessary boundaries will come off as too mean, will cause disruption in your relationships, or will be portrayed as selfish, you are not alone. While I can't guarantee that boundary-setting will be smooth sailing for everyone, here are a few ideas to set yourself up for success in establishing boundaries.

Suppose you've realized that your relationship with a childhood friend is a bit unbalanced, as you always drop everything to come to their rescue, but they are less than reliable when you need help. This is a classic dynamic that many of us find ourselves in at some point in life. Although the relationship may have started off more balanced, the current pattern leads you to feeling resentful, taken for granted, and maybe even a little worried about losing the friendship altogether.

A possible internal boundary, depending on the circumstance, could be, "I won't adopt their problems as my own or feel responsible for fixing everything." Now, this doesn't mean that you adopt a strict "that's a *you* problem" mentality. Jumping from overly involved to completely absent doesn't invite the balance you might be needing in these types of relationships. Instead, this sort of internal boundary helps create a reasonable degree of separation allowing you to support from an outside role rather than joining in and recreating the friend's firsthand distress within yourself.

If the initial internal boundary was not enough to make a noticeable shift in the dynamic, a similar expressed boundary might be something like, "I care about you and I value our friendship, *and* I'm hoping we can make our support of one another feel more balanced rather than one-sided." That's not too scary, right? You're not bluntly demanding for them to step up to the plate (unless that fits within your style of communication, of course). You are gently, but firmly, expressing your wants and needs to the other party in a way that might feel approachable for you if the roles were reversed.

The key to implementing expressed boundaries is to be clear and firm while remaining respectful. If you happen to be more of a people-pleaser, try to avoid over-explaining your boundaries or apologizing for them. Clarity and directness work in your favor when it comes to helping the other person understand that the boundary is important to you. That said, if the other person could benefit from learning more about why the boundary is needed or what it entails, providing extra context or information could be useful.

It is totally normal to feel guilty or hesitant at the start of your experience in implementing boundaries. If you're used to prioritizing others, shifting to prioritizing yourself will feel uncomfortable. Keep in mind, however, that the right boundaries will help healthy relationships flourish.

You might be wondering, "Okay, that sounds great, but what if the other person doesn't like my boundaries?" The hard truth is that a negative reaction is always a possibility. However, it's also good data. Some people might push back or resist when you try to implement a new boundary. This is especially the case when the other person has benefitted from your previous lack of boundaries. In circling back to the friendship example, someone who had access to an on-call crisis manager might be annoyed when asked to give support back. As you receive this data, you're better able to understand your friend's motivations and if this type of friendship is one you want to continue.

On the other hand, the negative reaction might give you insight on viewpoints that were missing. The friend could point out that they always want to support you when you need help, but at the same time you never express when you need it. Being open to a narrative shift in response to your boundary-setting could lead to beautiful and healing conversations for each party involved.

As you move forward with your chosen boundaries, keep yourself accountable in staying consistent with them. If you have expressed your boundary but fail to follow through with its execution, others might not take it seriously. You might even be undermining future boundaries by giving the impression that you're more bark than bite, so to speak.

Again, you're likely to encounter some bumps in the road as you practice boundary setting. Setting boundaries and following through with them can be intimidating at the start. Luckily, as you get more practice and confidence in standing up for your values and needs, the practice gets easier and you start to see the positive outcomes from your established boundaries.

EXERCISE 10.3 BOUNDARY IMPLEMENTATION PLAN

Choose one boundary to practice this week:

Is this internal or expressed?

If expressed, who do I need to communicate this to?

How will I phrase this boundary?

Potential pushback I might receive:

How I'll respond to pushback:

How I'll stay consistent with this boundary:

What support do I need to maintain this boundary?

The "Roundabout Boundary" for Beginners

If all else fails, let me share a brilliant hack I learned from one of my clients. As someone who is a generous giver and also *very* overcommitted, this client stumbled upon an easy way to avoid saying "no" or setting a direct boundary for incoming requests in a way that was not grating to her innate people-pleasing tendencies. In short, she says, "I need to check my schedule and I'll get back to you."

The power in this statement, as well as similar ones, is that it gives you time to figure out what to do. As an added bonus, you see the level of importance of the demand based on how the person responds. More often than not, you'll likely get a response of, "That's okay. If you're busy I can check with someone else." I view this interaction almost as a tango of people-pleasers, because people naturally want to avoid burdening others. By giving a non-committal answer, you get to move the people-pleasing responsibility back to the original asker. Or conversely, if they respond with, "Sure, let me know your availability because it's really important," you get insight on the value of the request based on the external information instead of just your base assumption.

Luckily this technique can be boiled down to a simple "I need to check" that can be applied to most types of expressed boundaries. You need to check your bank account, your carpool schedule, or your established commitments with others. If you decide to start out with the "roundabout boundary" style at first, you'll be able to get good practice in and gain comfort in standing up for yourself when it's time to move to more specific or direct boundaries.

Cultural Considerations

We can't conclude our conversation on boundaries without acknowledging how culture influences our relationships. The above classic approach to boundaries are admittedly designed to largely cater to Western and individualistic societies. Dare I say that they're most effective, and needed, within capitalistic societies, where "time is money" attitudes meet a culture that prioritizes self over community. As a result, these types of boundaries are likely to be grating to individuals operating in collectivistic communities.

In collectivistic cultures, cohesion and roles within groups like families and even society at large are prioritized over individual needs. Many Asian, Middle Eastern, African, and Latin American cultures work best when there is harmony within interdependent roles. Focusing on individual-prioritizing boundaries, like emphasizing, "Hey I won't be contributing to family dinner anymore because it's too demanding with my work schedule," could be seen as selfish and disrespectful in a way that fundamentally harms the relationship—and your health. Instead, look for boundaries that can be reframed around family or group well-being. You can also inch slowly toward changes to see how they impact both yourself and the larger group. Maybe, "I'll help with drinks and setting the table so that I can preserve my energy for work the next day and provide financially for the family" will work better for everyone involved.

Due to the prevalence of individual roles within a collectivistic culture, many of these communities also practice hierarchy and authority within interpersonal interactions. Elders and family or community leaders are to be respected. Saying "no" to grandma could become a disrupting interaction that ends up impacting the entire family system. Direct refusal could be particularly damaging in cultures or family systems that have an emphasis on obedience. Softening the language might work better in your favor. Saying "I appreciate your knowledge, thank you for your advice and I'll think about it," could land better in interactions with those in a higher authority than you.

There are also general communication styles to take into account when it comes to healthy boundaries. While some cultures prefer direct communication with assertive boundary-setting, others tend to practice indirect communication that implies boundaries instead of stating them outright. Countries like the Netherlands have language that is more straight-to-the-point, while speaking with others in Japan or Mexico means you might be using more subtle cues. I've found that there can also be a mix, particularly in cultures with hierarchy structures. Take Pakistan, for example. Speaking in Urdu, one of the many languages spoken in Pakistan, means you are making requests of others with very little "fluffy" fillers that can be found in English. This was quite a shock to my system when I moved to Pakistan and found none of the "would you mind..." or "I would appreciate it if you could..." statements that are more common in American Southern culture. That said, there is a different level of respect in the language and softer ways to word requests when speaking to elders in Pakistan.

What's the overall takeaway for setting boundaries that are culturally appropriate? When I meet with clients for the first time, I always emphasize that they are the experts in themselves. You are the person who best understands what you need, what type of environment you are in, and how you might be able to approach boundaries for your specific circumstances. Boundary advice you see online usually uses a one-size-fits-all approach, but we're all different shapes. Implement what works for you and get creative with what doesn't work from traditional boundary approaches.

EXERCISE 10.4 CULTURAL & PERSONAL CONTEXT

Boundaries in my culture look like:

In my family/culture, saying no is typically:
- Direct and acceptable
- Something that needs to be softened
- Generally discouraged
- Depends on who I'm talking to

A communication style that works best in my context:
- Direct and assertive
- Gentle and indirect
- Depends on the relationship

Adjustments I need to make to standard boundary advice:

Boundaries that align with my cultural background:

Creating Conditions for Connection and Respect

Learning to establish and maintain healthy boundaries is one of the most valuable investments you can make for your mental health and relationships. While the process can feel uncomfortable at first, especially if you're accustomed to prioritizing others' needs over your own, remember that boundaries aren't walls meant to keep people out. They're more like gates that help you control what enters your space and when. This creates the conditions for authentic connection and mutual respect to thrive.

The process of developing healthy boundaries is ongoing. It will evolve as you grow and your life circumstances change. What feels like an appropriate boundary in your twenties might need adjustment in your forties, and that's perfectly normal. The key is to remain attuned to your own needs while staying open to feedback and course-correction. Remember that boundaries aren't an excuse to avoid the equally important work of developing emotional self-regulation and communication skills. They work best when combined with genuine effort to understand others' perspectives and manage your own emotional responses.

As you continue building these skills, you're likely to find that the relationships in your life become more balanced, fulfilling, and sustainable. You'll create space for both your authentic self and meaningful connections with others.

EXERCISE 10.5 BOUNDARY GOALS & SELF-COMPASSION

My boundary goals for the next month:
(Up to three)

How I'll practice self-compassion as I learn:
- Remember this is a skill that takes time
- Celebrate small wins
- Not judge myself for past lack of boundaries
- Expect some discomfort

Signs that my boundaries are working:

Red flags that I might need professional help:
- Extreme guilt about any boundary setting
- Unable to say no in any situation
- Relationships becoming abusive when I set boundaries
- Complete social isolation due to rigid boundaries

My "roundabout" boundary phrases to practice:
- *I need to check my schedule and get back to you.*
- *Let me think about that and I'll let you know.*
- *I need to check with_____ first.*

Chapter 11

Understanding Stress and Its Impact

Unless you're a fan of surprises, you're likely keeping an eye on the changes of weather at the start of each day. Are there clear skies, thunderclouds on the horizon, wild winds, or predictions of snow? Weather is always present in some form, constantly changing and impacting our day—just like stress, which always has an underlying presence in the best of times and an overwhelming one in the worst of times. Just as we wouldn't expect to live in a world without changing weather, we can't realistically live a life completely free of stress. So, the healthiest and most sustainable goal isn't to eliminate stress entirely, but to understand it better and learn how to work with it as it shapeshifts throughout our days.

In this chapter, we'll explore what stress really is (beyond just feeling "stressed out"), how it manifests uniquely for each of us, and the impact it can have on both our minds and bodies. If you already know that stress plays a big part in your life—or if you realize its effect on you as you read through this chapter—keep note of the knowledge contained here since it lays the foundation for all the techniques we'll explore in later chapters. After all, you can't effectively manage something you don't understand.

The Stress Spectrum & Where You Land

Different Types of Stress

How often are you telling others that you're feeling stressed, and how often do you hear the people around you express that *they* are? With high-pressure work environments, constant economic and political changes, and increased difficulty to make time for self-care activities, I'd be surprised if you went a single day without the sentiment of stress being discussed. But when we talk about stress, we're often telling just part of the story while missing important nuances.

Stress comes in different forms and each one affects us in unique ways. When I'm sitting down with a client, I try to assess their experience of two specific types: eustress and distress. I'm ever the optimist so let's start by defining our dear friend *eustress*, a.k.a. the healthy stress response. Eustress is the positive tension that motivates and energizes us; it's the flutter of excitement at the start of a romantic relationship, the nervousness that sharpens your focus before giving a presentation, or the challenging deadline that helps you get down to business and produce your best work.

Distress, on the other hand, is the negative stress that causes anxiety and exceeds your perceived ability to cope. When you're experiencing distress, your nervous system becomes activated in a way that might not be so helpful in the moment. You'll likely notice thought patterns, such as catastrophization, leading to physiological changes, like increased sweat or heart palpitations. These are great responses when we're in imminent danger, but can be hindering when you're trying to navigate nerve-wracking situations like your first ever job interview. The three main categories within distress are: acute stress, episodic acute stress, and chronic stress—pretty much ranging from "bad" to "worst."

Acute Stress. *Acute stress* is typically a short-term stress response that happens in the face of an immediate threat or challenge. Sometimes it can heighten your senses when you need them the most, like when you're about to get in a car accident and your heart starts racing but your instinct to use defensive driving techniques kicks in. Other times, acute stress just makes you feel like your mind is jumbled. Like when you sat down for your physics exam in high school and felt as if your brain had suddenly forgotten all of the terminology from the entire semester. (Or was that just me?)

Episodic Acute Stress. You might guess by the name, but *episodic acute stress* is what happens when those episodes, or moments, of feeling of acute stress occur on a more regular basis. That car-accident-near-miss feeling becomes your everyday experience, and you start to live in crisis mode. You're running late, missing deadlines, and constantly putting out fires. If you've ever known someone who seems to attract drama wherever they go, or if you're that person yourself (no judgment here), then you're familiar with episodic acute stress. It's like living with your internal smoke alarm constantly blaring, even when there's no actual fire.

Chronic Stress. While *chronic stress* is also an ongoing experience, it's more of a slow burn. Having to navigate even low-level stressors on a regular basis can make stress feel so familiar that you might stop recognizing it as stress at all. Financial struggles, unhappy relationships, and soul-crushing jobs are all common experiences that have led us to accepting chronic stress as a normal experience. But just because something is common doesn't mean it's harmless. Burnout is the typical destination for anyone who experiences chronic stress and is unable or unwilling to make positive changes.

The funny thing about identifying the type of stress you're experiencing is that people have different tolerance levels for the same stressor. One person might feel energizing eustress around an upcoming presentation, while it causes debilitating distress for their colleague. Understanding your personal relationship with different types of stress is the first step toward working with them more effectively. (Chu et al., 2024)

Stress Intensity Scale

I won't lie, therapists love scaling questions, as they help transform subjective experiences to objective data. Scaling questions are also insanely easy for anyone to use. On a scale of 1 to 10, how much do you like pasta? Would you rate your swimming skills closer to a 1 or a 5, and why? And as you're reading this sentence, how would you rate the level of stress that you feel in your body from a scale of 1 to 10?

Most of us recognize stress only when it's hitting crisis levels, which is pretty much the equivalent of just noticing rain once you're caught in a thunderstorm without an umbrella. But developing awareness of your personal stress levels on a scale allows you to catch stress as it's still building, and therefore possibly mitigate it. When you're at the beginning of measuring, I typically suggest that a 1 is the lowest level and 10 is the highest. For example, a stress level of 3 might manifest as a slight tightness in your facial muscles, while a 7 could involve racing thoughts and a nervous stomach.

Those subtle early warning signs are your body's equivalent of distant thunder. It signals that a storm might be brewing and it's time to take precautions. Maybe your patience shortens, or you find yourself sighing more frequently, or your handwriting gets a little messier. These personalized stress indicators vary widely between individuals, which is why developing your own awareness is so crucial. If you're able to catch yourself at a level 2, for example, you'll find it easier to use far more interventions than when you hit a level 8 or 9.

Beyond being able to identify and therefore avoid overwhelmingly high stress levels, understanding where you fall on the stress intensity scale can help you healthily engage in eustress and boost your performance. For some, the sweet spot for experiencing eustress might be a 3 to 4 on the stress scale; for others who thrive under pressure, it might be a 5 to 6. Knowing your optimal zone helps you make better decisions about which challenges to take on and which ones to decline, as well as when.

EXERCISE 11.1 BUILDING YOUR PERSONAL STRESS SCALE

Define your stress levels by describing what each one feels like for you.

Level 1-2 (Minimal stress): Physical sensations? Thoughts? Emotions? Behaviors?

Level 3-4 (Low stress): Physical sensations? Thoughts? Emotions? Behaviors?

Level 5-6 (Moderate stress): Physical sensations? Thoughts? Emotions? Behaviors?

Level 7-8 (High stress): Physical sensations? Thoughts? Emotions? Behaviors?

Level 9-10 (Crisis stress): Physical sensations? Thoughts? Emotions? Behaviors?

Current stress level:

Optimal eustress zone (where I perform best):

Your Individual Stress Response Pattern

Because everyone has a different tolerance level for stress, plus varying responses even to the same triggers, it's important to not just track your stress scale, but also truly understand your own stress response pattern. Right now, a mystery stressor could come into your life and lead to emotional imbalance, ineffective thought patterns, and even damaging behaviors. Or the stress might find a way to show up in your body and make you feel not so great. But when you are able to identify the stressors that are unique to you, and recognize how that stress impacts your thoughts, feelings, and behaviors, you'll have the first skill in place to take a step back from the stress and make a more informed decision to move forward.

For example, after enduring a stressful political event recently, I felt chest pains for four days and hibernated for about 12 hours for three nights in a row. Let's not forget my daily emotional-support ice cream until the external stress settled down.

When I tuned into what was happening, it helped me recognize what had caused my stress and what I might want to set different boundaries against in the future.

Let's take a quick walk down memory lane and review the correlating factors as it specifically applies to stress. Identifying your stress triggers is the easiest way to prevent a stress spiral—when the trigger sets off a chain of stress response events in your mind and body that are harder to control. External factors are typically simpler to identify, like an argument with a loved one or bad traffic when you're already running late. When you're able to take a pause and say "Oh wow, this is a stress trigger for me," you're already on your way to being able to objectively observe the stress factor with some distance instead of getting completely immersed in it.

Internal stress triggers can be a bit more sneaky. Perfectionism, fear of failure, impostor syndrome, and catastrophic thinking are all powerful generators of internal stress. Interactions that poke at painful memories could also be triggers, like a colleague using the same tone of voice a parent did when you were being punished. Keep in mind too that your own thoughts, expectations, and self-imposed standards can generate significant stress without any external pressure. Even when there's no immediately endangering event, your body responds to thought-related stress the same way it does when you are actually experiencing the scenario. Creating a comprehensive personal stress trigger inventory means looking beyond the obvious to uncover these deeper patterns and associations.

If identifying a stressor feels like a difficult place to start, then try instead to notice when your body might be experiencing stress. Physical responses to stress are often the most noticeable signals that something's amiss. For example, your body might develop tension in specific areas—perhaps your shoulders rise up to your ears, your jaw clenches, or your chest feels tight. (I even had one client whose achy knees indicated the first signs of stress!) Even just shifting energy patterns can mean you're feeling stress. While some people become hyperactive as a stress response for example, others could suddenly feel drained. Insomnia or the desire to sleep all day could be other indicators. These physical manifestations are all your body's way of waving a red flag, alerting you to pay attention.

EXERCISE 11.2 STRESS TRIGGER & RESPONSE MAPPING

My top three external stress triggers:

My top three internal stress triggers:

My typical stress response pattern is:
- Fight (confrontational, aggressive)
- Flight (avoid, escape)
- Freeze (paralyzed, can't act)
- Fawn (people-please, appease)

Early warning signs my body gives me.
- Physical:
- Emotional:
- Behavioral:

When I'm stressed, I tend to:
- Overthink everything
- Make impulsive decisions
- Withdraw from others
- Become irritable
- Procrastinate
- Seek control

The Impact of Stress

The Brain and Nervous System

We feel stress physically because it has a direct impact on our nervous system—the network of nerves that extends throughout our entire bodies. Just as physical pain can send a message up to our brain through the nervous system, mental pain can send similar messages. The part of your nervous system most correlated with your psychology is the sympathetic nervous system—your body's built-in alarm system that has been honed throughout human history and evolution, designed to keep you safe from threats. Though we may not be running from saber-tooth tigers anymore, our sympathetic nervous system is still at the ready and on the lookout for potential harm.

This ancient stress response system now struggles in the modern world because it can't distinguish the difference between physical threats and psychological ones. Your body responds to an angry email with the same stress response as it would a physical attack. Financial worries, problems at work, and deliveries stolen off your front porch all set off a system of survival mechanisms designed for ancient life-or-death situations. But the stress response of our ancestors evolved for short-term challenges that would resolve quickly: either you escaped the predator or you didn't. It wasn't designed for the ongoing, persistent stressors of today that may last for months or years. Now it's like the car alarm that's supposed to be anti-theft but ends up blaring if a passerby accidently bumps it on the way to their own car.

Any level of stress is going to activate the sympathetic nervous system to some degree, meaning that your stress hormones will increase and you might even find yourself in fight, flight, freeze, or fawn mode. Some people naturally lean towards *fight*: becoming confrontational or aggressive when stressed. Others default to *flight*: avoiding conflict or literally removing themselves from stressful situations. The *freeze* response manifests as feeling paralyzed or unable to take action, while *fawn* involves people-pleasing and attempting to appease perceived threats. These are all different survival strategies your nervous system has learned over time. Understanding your typical pattern helps you recognize when your ancient survival mechanisms are running the show instead of your calmer, more rational mind.

When it comes to your brain and sympathetic nervous system, stress dramatically affects different regions, temporarily changing how you think and perceive the world. Your prefrontal cortex, responsible for rational thinking, planning, and impulse control, becomes less active when you're stressed. (This explains why you might say or do things in the heat of the moment that you later regret.) Meanwhile, your amygdala, the brain's threat detection center, becomes more active and makes you more reactive to potential dangers. This results in being more likely to interpret even harmless situations negatively.

These brain changes impact your memory, learning, and decision-making in significant ways. When you're experiencing higher levels of stress, your brain prioritizes immediate survival information (where the closest shelter is) over details it deems less important for survival (whether you have green beans or broccoli sitting in your fridge). So, you might forget someone's name moments after being introduced at a stressful networking event, or you could struggle to recall information during a high-pressure exam despite knowing it perfectly well while studying. Similarly, when under even mild stress, decision-making becomes more impulsive and short-term focused. Evolutionarily, this makes sense. Why do any long-term planning when running from a predator? In everyday situations, however, this kind of short-term thinking creates problems if you're attempting to make discerning choices about relationships, finances, or your career.

EXERCISE 11.3 STRESS IMPACT ASSESSMENT

How stress currently impacts my:

Physical health
- Sleep problems
- Headaches
- Muscle tension
- Digestive issues
- Fatigue
- Frequent illness

Mental functioning
- Forgetfulness
- Difficulty concentrating
- Poor decision-making
- Racing thoughts
- Mental fog

Emotional well-being
- Irritability
- Anxiety
- Mood swings
- Feeling overwhelmed

- Low mood
- Emotional numbness

Relationships
- More conflict
- Withdrawing from others
- Less patience
- Difficulty communicating

Work/productivity
- Missing deadlines
- Lower quality work
- Procrastination
- Difficulty prioritizing

Cumulative Effects of Stress

What we've talked about so far in this chapter are the generally-obvious short-term effects of stress: the racing heart, reactivity, sweaty palms, muscle tension, forgetfulness, or heightened alertness that signal your body's alarm system has activated. These short-term effects can be useful in truly threatening situations, helping you respond effectively to danger. If you're about to miss your bus and the panic in your body temporarily diverts resources to your muscles and heightens your senses, you're more likely to catch your bus and return to normal functioning once you're sitting in that bus seat.

I'm more concerned about my clients' chronic stress and the toll it can take on their mental and physical health. The best way I can describe this cumulative impact is similar to the way water slowly erodes a rock over time. You might not, for example, connect your gradually increasing blood pressure, slowly expanding waistline, or progressively worsening sleep quality with the ongoing stress in your life. These changes often happen so incrementally that they become your "new normal," making them harder to recognize and address.

Individual stressors might also seem manageable on their own (the slightly too-long commute, the mildly difficult coworker, the somewhat cramped living space), but cumulatively they create a total stress load that exceeds your capacity to recover fully. This is why sometimes adding what seems like a minor additional responsibility to your daily to-do list can suddenly make everything feel overwhelming. It's not that you can't handle that task on its own; it's that your stress cup was already filled to the brim and even one more drop causes an overflow.

As Dr. Gabor Maté describes in his book *When the Body Says No* (2003), a stress cup that's constantly full and overflowing can lead to chronic physical health issues. Your cardiovascular, immune, and digestive systems for example are more susceptible to damage from intense and prolonged stress. A constant flood of stress hormones can therefore increase the risk of conditions like cardiovascular disease, digestive complications, and autoimmune disorders.

If you're now realizing that your stress levels are pretty high on a regular basis, does this mean you are destined for a chronic disease? Fortunately, the answer is no! How we experience stress can be managed, allowing us to modulate the psychological and physical stress response chain of events. As you build up your skills to observe and distance yourself from the stressors in your life, you'll also be able to respond more appropriately in a way that sets you up for mental and physical health.

Prepping for Stress Management

Stress management is a practice, not a destination. Managing stress effectively is a lifelong practice that evolves with changing circumstances. This practice mindset removes the pressure of "solving" stress once and for all (an impossible goal) and focuses instead on developing skills you can apply throughout your life to handle it differently over time. Some days your practice will feel easier and more effective than others, and that variation is completely normal.

I know I keep repeating this idea, but the importance of personalization when it comes to stress relief cannot be overstated. Despite what clickbait-using wellness influencers might suggest, there is no universal "best" stress management technique that works perfectly for everyone. What calms one person might irritate another. The weekly massage that your friend swears by might amplify your financial stress. The still-and-silent meditation practice that I love makes my husband feel restless and agitated. Stress management isn't about following prescriptive rules but is instead about discovering what actually works for your unique nervous system, preferences, and circumstances.

Building your own personalized toolkit of stress responses will involve experimentation and honest self-assessment. As you work through the next chapters, pay attention to which practices resonate more strongly with you, and adapt the others to better suit your needs. My goal here is to help you develop a diverse repertoire of strategies you can draw upon flexibly depending on the type and intensity of stress you're experiencing.

EXERCISE 11.4 STRESS MANAGEMENT READINESS

Current coping strategies I use:
- Exercise
- Talking to friends/family
- Deep breathing
- Distraction
- Alcohol/substances
- Sleeping
- Eating more/less
- Working more
- Using social media
- Shopping

Which of these strategies actually help?

Which strategies make things worse?

Stress management approaches I'm curious about:
- Mindfulness/meditation
- Physical exercise
- Creative activities
- Time management
- Boundary setting
- Professional help

Barriers to stress management for me:
- Time constraints
- Not knowing what works
- Feeling guilty taking time
- Financial limitations
- Not believing it'll help

My motivation for better stress management:

Strategic Stress Management

Understanding stress is a great first step towards building an effective stress management system. Stress exists on a spectrum from helpful eustress to overwhelming distress, and we each have different definitions as to how we categorize different stressors. Learning trapeze arts may fall under the distress scale for me, while the same activity could be a riveting eustress experience for passionate acrobats. By developing awareness of your personal stress patterns and triggers, you've taken the most crucial step towards identifying managing stress more skillfully. The goal isn't to eliminate stress entirely, which would be neither possible nor beneficial, but to develop a more informed and intentional relationship with it.

The cumulative effects of chronic stress on your body and mind underscores why this understanding matters so much. Your nervous system's design for short-term physical threats can often misinterpret modern psychological stressors as life-or-death situations, creating wear and tear on your body's systems that can lead to real health consequences over time. That said, the nervous system is also resilient and has remarkable capacity for shifting and healing when you work with it rather than against. By incorporating stress management skills when you first notice signs of stress, you're able to re-train your body's typical responses to stress.

We'll explore and build upon the self-awareness around stress that you've developed thus far. Just as your stress response is unique to you—shaped by your biology, personal history, and current circumstances—your toolkit for managing stress should be equally individualized. If you're feeling armed with knowledge about your personal stress patterns, optimal stress zones, and early warning signals, then now would be a great time to start experimenting with specific techniques to foster growth and re-silience. Stress management can evolve throughout your life, just as most well-being practices do, so staying in tune with your mind and body's stress levels and being flexible with trying new skills can only help set you up for success.

EXERCISE 11.5 STRESS MANAGEMENT READINESS

My priority area for stress management:
- Reducing overall stress levels
- Improving stress recognition
- Building better coping skills
- Addressing chronic stressors
- Learning prevention strategies

One specific stress trigger I want to work on:

My stress management goal for next month:

Support I might need:
- Professional counseling
- Medical consultation
- Friend/family support
- Stress management resources
- Lifestyle changes

How I'll track my progress:
- Daily stress level rating
- Symptom tracking
- Mood journal
- Sleep/energy monitoring

Warning signs that I need immediate professional help:
- Chronic insomnia
- Panic attacks
- Substance use increase
- Thoughts of self-harm
- Complete inability to function

Chapter 12

Relaxation Techniques and Stress Relief

Now that you've gained insight on your personal stress response and understand the biology behind stress, you're ready to begin transforming your relationship with it. Think of Chapter 11 as the prescription phase. You've identified where you hold tension, recognized your early warning signs, and know more about your stress patterns. This chapter marks the transition from awareness to action.

Relaxation techniques are your mental health first-aid kit—simple yet powerful tools that can bring your nervous system back into balance when stress has you feeling overwhelmed. But relaxation is more than just a simple counter to immediate stress. When practiced regularly, these techniques can actually reshape your baseline stress levels, creating a more resilient nervous system that doesn't get activated as easily in the first place. It's like strengthening your immune system rather than just treating symptoms after you get sick.

In this chapter, we'll explore a variety of evidence-based relaxation methods, help you find the ones that resonate with your unique needs, and show you how to weave them seamlessly into your daily life—no expensive vacation required. (Unless you already have a trip booked, then vacation away!) The techniques in this chapter are all proven to help you find calm amidst chaos. You might have heard of some, but never fully given them a go because of internal doubt or lack of time in your schedule. But I'm here to once again encourage you to try to curb any eye rolls, and give these techniques the good 'ol college try—with intentionality and regular scheduled time to practice them—because they really do work.

The Science of Relaxation

Your relaxation response is essentially the opposite of the stress response we explored in Chapter 11. While your stress response activates your sympathetic nervous system (increasing heart rate, blood pressure, and muscle tension), the relaxation response engages your parasympathetic nervous system, creating a cascade of calming physiological changes. Your heart rate slows, your blood pressure decreases, your breathing deepens, and your muscles release their tension (Evans-Martin, 2022). You're essentially flipping the switch from panic to peace.

Scientists refer to the parasympathetic nervous system as your "rest and digest" or "tend and befriend" system because it's your body's built-in calming mechanism. While your sympathetic nervous system prepares you for action in the face of threat, your parasympathetic system promotes recovery, healing, and social connection. The beauty of relaxation techniques is that they purposefully activate this parasympathetic response and give you a degree of control over what is typically an automatic process. Rather than waiting for your body to calm down naturally (which might take hours or days), these practices allow you to initiate the calming process intentionally and immediately.

Your relaxation response, similar to the stress response, also can show up in *acute* (very short-term and temporary) or *chronic* activity (on an ongoing, long-term basis). Regular relaxation practice creates lasting neurological changes through *neuroplasticity*, your brain's ability to reorganize itself by forming new neural connections. The more you practice relaxation exercises, the easier it is for your brain to choose a relaxation response over a stress response. Practicing relaxation for just 10 to 15 minutes a day can build up to long-term changes for your brain and nervous system.

Not only does strengthening your relaxation skills help you better cope with immediate stressors, but it also helps you function better in other areas of your life. Contrary to the productivity culture myth that suggests stress and pressure are needed for peak performance, chronic stress actually impairs cognitive function and work quality. A moderately relaxed state is proven to be optimal for most cognitive tasks, creative work, and decision-making. These aren't nice-to-have bonuses; they're substantial performance enhancements that directly impact your effectiveness in work and life.

As a result, more and more often we are now seeing typically high-pressure work environments adopting measures to ensure employees are able to reduce stress. This isn't coincidental, or even out of the kindness of their corporate hearts. Rather it's because research consistently shows that breaks from stress improve performance, which is great for company success. That's why many large companies have wellness programs, and high-value companies like Google have nap pods and even meditation and gaming rooms available for employees.

Relaxation Roadblocks

If relaxation is so great, why aren't we doing it? There are three main objections I hear in therapy when we talk about taking time to relax:

1. I don't have time.

2. I don't want to be lazy, and

3. What if I let everything go and can't function after?

I myself am familiar with all three of these! These days I typically fall back on the excuse of not having time to relax. Trust me, I'd love to park myself on the couch for a few hours but the demands of family life usually have me hopping back on my feet after a few seconds of rest. Or, if I think about relaxing knowing I have overdue tasks hanging over my head, guilt creeps in and I find myself making my way to my desk. The fear of letting too much go is particularly potent for those of us who are Type A and lean toward perfectionism. It can be hard to release the demands of the day if we don't trust ourselves to get back up for the grind after hitting pause on the flow of momentum.

My solution is to be strategic about relaxation. Start small with just 5 to 10 minutes of intentional practice, and have these few minutes scheduled around another task you typically complete during the day with no problem. For example, when I work with Muslim clients, I suggest practicing relaxation in the couple of minutes before praying. If you're a coffee drinker, take a second to relax while your coffee is brewing. These practices are short-term enough to evade feelings of shame in response to perceived "laziness," while also incorporating buffer activities that prevent you from "falling apart" as you find your relaxation footing.

Many people also give up on relaxation techniques because they don't experience immediate benefits, or feel they're "doing it wrong" when their mind wanders. This would be like going to the gym once, lifting a weight incorrectly and straining a muscle, and then concluding that "exercise doesn't work for me." (Which, to be fair, I have definitely been guilty of in the past.) Like any skill worth developing, relaxation techniques become more effective with consistent practice. Activities that at first feel awkward or only minimally helpful can often become the most powerful tools in your stress management toolkit over time. I struggled with silent meditations when I first started out, usually preferring guided audio meditations, but now find that I can sit comfortably and powerfully in silence for hours on end. That is, if I don't happen to fall asleep while feeling so relaxed.

Your optimal balance between tension and relaxation will be unique to you. A concert pianist needs enough activation to energize their performance, but enough relaxation to not get frozen at the keys. A surgeon needs focused attention and steady hands—skills and traits requiring both alertness and calmness simultaneously. Your optimal zone might differ based on the task you're undertaking, your personality, and even the time of day based on how rested or drained you are. Throughout this chapter, we'll work to identify your personal sweet spot in balancing healthy stress with relaxation.

EXERCISE 12.1 RELAXATION ROADBLOCKS ASSESSMENT

What typically stops me from relaxing?
- Don't have time
- Feel guilty/lazy
- Don't know how
- Fear of losing control
- Too restless
- Mind races
- Feel it's not important
- Other responsibilities come first

When I try to relax, I usually:
- Fall asleep
- Get more anxious
- Start thinking about tasks
- Feel bored
- Feel physically uncomfortable
- Can't actually relax

My current "relaxation" activities:
- TV/streaming
- Scrolling social media
- Reading
- Bath/shower
- Music
- Exercise
- Sleep
- Alcohol/substances
- None, really

Which of these actually help me feel calmer?

My biggest obstacle to regular relaxation practice:

Realistic time I could commit to relaxation daily:

The Art of Tuning In
(and Rebrand of Mindfulness)

The base relaxation skill that I encourage all my clients to start with is *mindfulness*. Now, if you're like the majority of my clients, you may feel resistant and skeptical about the term "mindfulness," thanks to the pop psychology version of mindfulness that's come out over the past decade or so. I know, I know. It's like when you hear the same song on the radio all the time and eventually change the frequency whenever you get even a hint of that song starting.

So since the point of this chapter is to facilitate mental ease, let's reframe this skill here into "tuning in"—a name that better matches the action that you actually take when you practice it. Instead of simply going through the motions throughout your day and during interactions, "tuning in" is the non-judgmental skill of becoming aware of your experience in the present moment. It's noticing what's happening right now in your body, your thoughts, your emotions, and your surroundings. An important second step is to not get caught in judgments (also known as *secondary reactions*) about whether those experiences are good or bad, right or wrong. For now, you're simply observing yourself in a new way.

Sure, this may sound simple enough, but simple doesn't necessarily mean easy. So many of us are operating on autopilot throughout the day. We start to mindlessly scroll social media when we wake up, our minds stay in the past or in the future instead of in the present, or we react to the world around us without first fully checking in with ourselves. Being able to take the first step and pause at a time where you're usually swept up in the moment can be difficult.

A Pause of 60 Seconds

There are several ways to get the momentum going when trying to start tuning in. While some people are able to do so at any given moment, some of us need to build up to that ability. I love the easy practice of a one-minute tune-in. This can be done anywhere and anytime, to help you develop the skill consistently until it becomes second-nature.

At first, you may want to choose a specific time during the day, or even set a routine alarm each day, to pause whatever you're doing. You can start the one-minute tune in by taking three slow, deep breaths. Notice the physical sensations of breathing—the expansion and contraction of your chest, the temperature of the air, the movement of your body. Then bring your attention to any physical sensations present right now. Sense if there are any points of contact with the surfaces supporting you, any areas of tension or comfort, the air temperature, the sounds around you, etc. Finally, notice your current emotional state without trying to change it.

Before you even know it, bam! The 60 seconds are up and you can resume whatever you were doing. You might notice that your mind is a little clearer or you feel a bit more calm when coming back to the "real world." (Or you might not feel any difference, which is totally normal when you're first starting out.) The brief minute that you took to tune in with yourself and your surroundings interrupts your automatic pilot mode and reestablishes conscious presence. You're basically hitting the reset button on your attention and your intentional existence in the current moment.

Body Scanning

I'm also quite the fan of *body scanning*, which I often guide clients through in sessions. Body scanning entails bringing attention to different parts of your body, typically in the order from head to toe. You can do this by yourself, with a mental health professional, or even through guided audio or video. Starting at your head, mentally work your way down your body and notice different sensations. What temperature, pressure, tension, tingling, or other sensations are present? Where are sensations absent or difficult to detect?

This practice grounds you in physical rather than thought-based reality, and often reveals tension you weren't aware you were holding. You might naturally release this tension just by noticing it, or you can intentionally release it as your attention scans your body. For clients who have a difficult time releasing tension, I suggest doing a mental shake (literally imagining that you're shaking the tension out), or trying to tense the muscles in that area as much as you can before letting go and relaxing.

A Full Mental Picture

Tuning into your mind is similar to body scanning in that you're taking a moment to truly observe which thoughts are present in that moment. A classic exercise for tuning into your mind is a "leaves on the stream" exercise. Imagine sitting beside a stream, watching leaves float by on the current. Each leaf represents a thought, feeling, or sensation that arises in your awareness. Instead of jumping onto the leaf and being carried downstream (getting lost in the thought), you simply observe it passing by. When you notice you've been swept away by a thought—which happens to everyone—gently return to your observer position on the bank of the stream. This practice builds your *metacognition*, or the ability to observe your own thoughts, which will be critical later on down the line when you want to change unhelpful thought patterns.

Environmental Awareness

If exclusively tuning your attention inward causes any distress, you might want to flip the script and tune into your environment instead. I especially suggest this method to anyone who is naturally anxious and experiences panic. To tune into your environment, pick any one of your senses and give it your full attention for at least one minute. If you choose focusing on vision, you might fully observe a single object, noticing the details, colors, textures, and shadows you ordinarily overlook. For hearing, you could close your eyes and identify as many distinct sounds in your environment as possible. To concentrate on touch, you might fully experience the sensations of water on your hands while washing them.

Each of these practices help you more completely observe your inner and external experience, strengthening your ability to recognize stressors without getting too sucked into them, and more quickly return to a state of calm.

EXERCISE 12.2 MINDFULNESS PRACTICE LOG

Try each technique for two to three days and rate your experience. (1–5, 5 being helpful for relaxing)

60-second pause: Days practiced? Helpfulness? What I noticed?

Body scanning: Days practiced? Helpfulness? What I noticed?

Mental observation: Days practiced? Helpfulness? What I noticed?

Environmental awareness: Days practiced? Helpfulness? What I noticed?

Which technique felt most natural or effective?

Which was most challenging?

Best time of day for me to practice:

Breathwork

I hate to break it to you, but you might not be breathing right. (Just kidding, it's a great sign for you to be breathing at all right now!) The truth is that the way we breathe is strongly correlated to how we feel. There's a two-way street between our breathing patterns and our nervous system. When you're stressed, your breathing naturally becomes shallow, rapid, and chest-centered. Conversely, when you're relaxed, your breathing becomes deeper, slower, and stems from your abdomen. Breathing is a unique relaxation tool because you can deliberately use it to reverse your state.

By intentionally shifting your breathing pattern, you send signals to your brain that directly influences your nervous system. (Basically, you have a remote control for your own physiology!) There is unique power in breathwork because it allows you to take control of a system that is typically automatic. Unlike your heart rate or hormone levels, which are always automatic, your breathing has both automatic and voluntary modes. By voluntarily changing your breathing pattern, you can influence functions that are otherwise outside your conscious control, like heart rate, blood pressure, and stress hormone release.

Breathing is the fastest way to shift your physiological state because it directly impacts your vagus nerve, which is the primary nerve of your parasympathetic nervous system. Slow, deep breathing stimulates this nerve and triggers a cascade of calming effects throughout your body. While other physical and mental techniques also activate the relaxation response, breath-based approaches typically work more quickly and can create noticeable shifts in under two minutes. This makes breathing techniques particularly valuable for those acute stress situations when you need rapid relief.

Here are a few of my favorite breathing techniques:

Belly breathing. Also known as diaphragmatic breathing, this involves placing one hand on your chest and the other on your diaphragm. As you inhale slowly through your nose, feel your abdomen expand outward while your chest remains relatively still. As you exhale through your mouth, feel your abdomen contract. By fully engaging your diaphragm, you take in more oxygen and stimulate your vagus nerve.

4-7-8 breathing. Inhale quietly through your nose for a count of 4, hold your breath for a count of 7, then exhale completely through your mouth with a whooshing sound for a count of 8. The extended exhale is what stimulates your parasympathetic nervous system, creating a relaxation response that can be helpful for targeting acute stress, anxiety, and even insomnia.

Box breathing. Also known as square breathing, this involves an inhale for a count of 4, hold for 4, exhale for 4, and hold for 4. Repeat as needed. You can visualize tracing the sides of a square as you move through each phase. This breathing pattern helps regulate the autonomic nervous system and improves focus under pressure. Its simple counting pattern of 4s makes it easy to remember during stressful situations.

Alternate nostril breathing. Derived from a yoga tradition, this can be practiced by closing one nostril to inhale, then opening that nostril and closing the other to release the exhale. Repeat by inhaling through the nostril that was opened for your last exhale, and so on and so forth. Research shows this technique balances activity between the sympathetic and parasympathetic branches of your nervous system, making it particularly helpful for when you're "stuck" in a stress response.

The physiological sigh. This is my all-time favorite breathing technique because it's the easiest and I've seen it to be instantly effective for many of my clients. You start by taking a deep breath. Once you've filled your lungs, see if there's any room for just a little more air. (Like when people top off their gas tank at the pump.) After you've squeezed in all the air possible, slowly exhale through your mouth. Repeat as needed.

EXERCISE 12.3 BREATHING TECHNIQUE EXPLORATION

Try each technique and record your response, rating the difficulty level. (1 to 5, 5 being very difficult)

Belly Breathing: Immediate effect? Difficulty?

4-7-8 Breathing: Immediate effect? Difficulty?

Box Breathing: Immediate effect? Difficulty?

Alternate Nostril Breathing: Immediate effect? Difficulty?

Physiological Sigh: Immediate effect? Difficulty?

Beyond the Basics

If you've mastered the art of tuning in and breathwork, you can explore additional methods to further build your relaxation toolkit. Here are some physical, sensory-cased, and creative relaxation tools you can try out:

Progressive muscle relaxation. This is pretty much a body scan with the added step of tensing and releasing each muscle as you check in with your body from head to toe. Over time, you might even be able to automatically release the tension without having to clench any muscles.

Self-massage. Use gentle pressure to manually release tension in accessible areas. This works by increasing blood flow while stimulating sensory receptors that signal your brain to reduce muscle contraction. (And massages just generally feel pretty darn good.)

Relaxation-focused stretching. Focus on stretches that target your personal tension spots. Hold each stretch while breathing deeply and visualizing the muscle softening with each exhale.

Sound therapy. Different sounds affect your nervous system in predictable ways, with certain rhythms and frequency ranges consistently eliciting relaxation responses. Nature sounds like rainfall or ocean waves often work well because they combine rhythmic predictability with organic variability. Singing bowls, often used by sound therapists, create sound frequencies that promote alpha and theta brainwaves associated with relaxation and meditation. Even humming or singing can stimulate your vagus nerve through the vibrations created in your throat and chest.

Aromatherapy. Scents can trigger a relaxation effect through the olfactory system's connection to the same brain receptors that are targeted by anti-anxiety medications. Lavender, citrus, and rosemary are particularly known for their psychosomatic impact.

Visual relaxation. Watching slow-moving visual cues is a great activity to get our mind and body to start moving slower, too. If you are observing, or even imagining, fluffy clouds gliding through the sky, green leaves blowing in the wind, or the mesmerizing goo inside a lava lamp, you're able to shift your brain activity more towards relaxation. (I have literally encouraged clients to purchase lava lamps before; give it a try!)

Expressive arts. If you're an active person, you might like using sensory engagement, flow states, and emotional release through activities like painting, scrapbooking, and coloring. Yes, those adult coloring books actually work! The key here is to focus on the process instead of the product, creating without judgment.

EXERCISE 12.4 SPECIFIC RELAXATION SAMPLER

Rate your interest and experience with each.

Progressive Muscle Relaxation: Interest level? Tried it? Experience?

Self-Massage: Interest level? Tried it? Experience?

Relaxation-Focused Stretching: Interest level? Tried it? Experience?

Sound/Music Therapy: Interest level? Tried it? Experience?

Aromatherapy: Interest level? Tried it? Experience?

Visual Relaxation: Interest level? Tried it? Experience?

Expressive Arts: Interest level? Tried it? Experience?

Which techniques am I most curious to explore further?

What are potential barriers to trying these techniques?

Relaxation Sometimes Requires Practice

Relaxation shouldn't be a luxury—it's a biological reset that is the foundation for your basic functioning and well-being. Our nervous systems simply weren't designed for constant activation with minimal rest. Giving your mind and body the break it needs to recover boosts your resilience and lets you put your best foot forward.

Remember that relaxation is a skill that improves with practice. Don't be discouraged if some techniques feel awkward at first or if your mind wanders during practice. That's completely normal! Like any worthwhile skill, relaxation gets easier and more effective over time. Each time you practice, you're strengthening neural pathways that make the relaxation response more accessible in the future. Even "unsuccessful" practice sessions contribute to this neural strengthening, so there's truly no wasted effort.

As you move through the next few days, experiment with different approaches to find what resonates with your mind and body. Notice which techniques create the most demonstrative shifts for you personally. Pay attention to which practices you're naturally drawn to and which feel sustainable with your lifestyle and preferences. The most effective relaxation practice isn't the one that is most frequently discussed in pop psychology today; it's the one that you'll actually do consistently.

EXERCISE 12.5 PERSONAL RELAXATION TOOLKIT

Based on all my experimentation, my top three relaxation techniques are:

My relaxation schedule: (daily, weekly)
- Optimal conditions for my relaxation practice:
- Time of day:
- Location:
- Environment:

How I'll remember to practice:
- Phone reminder
- Calendar appointment
- Link to existing habit
- Relaxation buddy

Signs that my relaxation practice is working:

Adjustments I might need to make:

Support I might need:
- Guided audio/apps
- Professional instruction
- Practice partner
- Better environment setup

Chapter 13

Practicing Gratitude & Cognitive Reframing

Now that we're ready to ramp up from a foundation of relaxation, you can move on to two other stress reducers: focusing on gratitude and reframing. Rather than simply reducing negative mental states, these practices actively cultivate positive ones. We're not just removing weeds from a garden (stress management), but intentionally planting flowers as well (gratitude and cognitive reframing).

If Chapters 11 and 12 were about creating space and calm in your mental environment, this chapter is about what you can choose to fill that space with. When we're on autopilot, our minds have a natural tendency to lean toward problem-solving, threat detection, and critique. As we've discussed, these are all useful cognitive functions that were particularly handy when we were in early eras of mere survival as a species, but they become problematic when they occupy our minds excessively. The practices in this chapter offer a counterbalance to stress by intentionally directing your attention toward appreciation, possibility, and constructive interpretation.

For these exercises, we're going to draw from the fields of positive psychology and cognitive behavioral therapy, which are supported by research that has shown that these practices aren't just feel-good exercises but effective tools that create measurable changes in our brain wiring, thought patterns, and overall well-being (Nakao et al., 2021; Chiarrochi et al., 2022). The best part? They're surprisingly easy to learn. They just require consistent practice to create lasting change. Let's explore how purposefully shifting your focus toward gratitude and deliberately reframing negative thought patterns can transform your mental landscape, one thought at a time.

How It Works

Gratitude

When you consciously focus on things you appreciate, your brain produces the same "feel-good" chemicals it does when you've just received a gift or experienced success. This neurochemical response isn't momentary, either—with repeated practice, gratitude strengthens your neural pathways, making it easier for your brain to access positive emotions. It's like creating a well-traveled path through a forest; the more you walk it, the clearer and more accessible it becomes.

After repetition over time, your brain becomes more adept at noticing the positive aspects of your experience without conscious effort. This mindset shift gradually transforms from something you must do deliberately to a lens through which you naturally see the world. And moving through the world in this new way actually shapes how you feel. More than that, research findings around gratitude's impact on our psychology shows measurable improvement in sleep quality, lower stress levels, and increased mental resiliency (Newman et al., 2021). So, gratitude doesn't just feel good, but it creates tangible physical benefits, comparable to some health interventions.

Perhaps most surprisingly, gratitude works even when you don't "feel grateful" at first. (Which is likely most of us!) I was relieved to learn this, as clients often express hesitation to practice gratitude exercises because it "feels fake" or can seem cheesy when they first start out. Luckily, the intentional act of looking for things to appreciate, even when done mechanically at the outset, gradually generates authentic feelings of gratitude. This is because gratitude isn't just an emotion that either appears or doesn't; it's also a practice of focusing your attention that can be deliberately cultivated.

Cognitive Reframing

Cognitive reframing works in a similar manner, starting as an intentional thought that results in changed emotions and experiences. Employing different thought patterns around the same event can create entirely different emotional experiences, which means changing those patterns gives you significant influence over your emotional life.

For example, if you've ever received a text that says, "We need to talk tomorrow" from your boss or partner, you're probably familiar with how your interpretation of that message can influence your emotional response. If your brain is flooded with everything you could have possibly done wrong, you're likely to freak out and be a nervous wreck until you can get tomorrow's conversation over with. If you instead think about other topics they might bring up, like recognizing something great you did or asking you for help with an unexpected task, you're able to better manage your emotional response.

When you consistently practice looking at situations from different perspectives, you're literally rewiring your brain over time. Brain imaging studies show that consistent cognitive reframing practices can actually change the structure and function of brain regions involved in emotional regulation and executive function (Agathos, 2023). This means the prefrontal cortex (your brain's "rational manager") is able to strengthen its connections to the amygdala (your brain's "alarm system"), allowing for more thoughtful responses to potentially upsetting situations.

Getting Started with Gratitude

Practicing gratitude in a way that actually works requires a few key elements that are often missing from generic advice on the topic. First, you really need to establish a consistent time and place—perhaps with your morning coffee or just before bed—to minimize any decision fatigue and to build momentum through habit.

Second, determine your preferred format. Whether you want to write down what you're grateful for in a notebook or typed in an app—which I recommend—or if you want to start off simply in your mind, it's important to choose something you'll be able to repeat consistently.

Third, start listing your gratitudes with a manageable frequency. Doing so daily is ideal, but three times a week can still do the trick if that's more sustainable for you. Finally, commit to a minimum amount of practice during each sitting (recognizing three specific items) while giving yourself permission to continue if you're feeling inspired.

If you're feeling stuck or your practice is starting to feel dull or contrived, gratitude prompts are great for providing direction. Instead of simply listing anything you appreciate, prompts encourage deeper reflection on specific domains: "What relationship am I grateful for today and why?" or "What challenge am I facing that contains something to appreciate?" or "What sensory experience brought me joy today?" Using diverse prompts prevents your practice from becoming stale and helps you dig into the deeper layers of gratitude.

Making gratitude specific, fresh, and meaningful elevates your practice from a mechanical exercise to a genuinely beneficial routine. You want to be *specific* about what exactly you appreciate and why, as this creates stronger neural activation than vague entries. *Freshness* involves varying your focus instead of listing the same things repeatedly, which prevents hedonic adaptation (becoming numb to repeated positives). *Meaningfulness* comes from connecting your gratitude to your core values and relationships, rather than material possessions or surface pleasures. Incorporating all of these qualities transforms gratitude practice from a chore into a genuine exploration of what matters most to you.

A more specific guided practice for gratitude, and my personal favorite to use with clients, is the "Three Good Things" exercise. Not only is it super easy to implement, but it has a strong research backing, with studies showing it can decrease depression symptoms and increase happiness for up to three months after consistent practice (Gold et al., 2023). Here's what you do: Each night before bed, write down three good things that happened that day, along with a brief reflection on why each happened and what it means to you. That's it!

EXERCISE 13.1 A STARTER 3-DAY GRATITUDE PRACTICE

Day 1: Good thing? Why it happened? What it means?

Day 2: Good thing? Why it happened? What it means?

Day 3: Good thing? Why it happened? What it means?

After three days, how did this feel?

What made it easier/harder than expected?

Taking Gratitude to the Next Level

Moving beyond obvious gratitude to find subtler instances of appreciation takes your practice to a whole new level. Once you've covered the easy-to-identify sources of gratitude, like relationships, health, and material comforts, challenge yourself to notice less obvious gifts: the opportunity to take transportation to the beach even if it's far away from you, the perfect temperature of your shower, or the convenience of having information instantly available through the tiny computer in your pocket. Look for what author David Steindl-Rast (2013) calls the *gift of opportunity* of each moment, meaning that there's an opportunity to be grateful in any moment or experience. And such an opportunity is a gift in itself.

Practicing gratitude during challenging times often feels counterintuitive, but can be particularly transformative. This doesn't mean forcing gratefulness for the actual difficulties themselves, which would be *toxic positivity*, but rather staying aware of what still works amidst the struggle. When you're sick, for example, you might appreciate having healthcare access, a body that's fighting to heal, or even just a plentiful supply of tissues. During relationship conflict, you might acknowledge the opportunity for honesty the disagreement allows, or the values revealed by what matters enough to create strong feelings. This practice doesn't diminish the challenges you're experiencing, but provides a wider perspective that includes both struggle and support. This way, difficulties aren't consuming your entire attention.

EXERCISE 13.2 ADVANCED GRATITUDE CHALLENGE

Think of a current difficulty.

My current challenge:

What still works despite this challenge:

Opportunities this challenge might offer:

Support available to me during this:

The Art of Cognitive Reframing

The essential first step in reframing involves identifying your common negative thought loops. Most people have recurring patterns of unhelpful thinking that appear across different situations, like familiar but unwelcome visitors in your mind. Perhaps you easily jump to worst-case scenarios, assume others are judging you negatively, or mentally replay embarrassing moments. (Thanks a lot, brain). As with "tuning in" relaxation techniques in Chapter 12, we want to first notice these patterns without judgment. Consider keeping a thought log for a few days to identify recurring themes, paying particular attention to thoughts that are accompanied by strong emotions or those that seem to pop up automatically without direct intention. Building this awareness creates the necessary space between you and your thoughts for reframing to become possible.

Once you're in this habit, to better discern which thoughts to reframe and which you can leave as they are, there's one distinction to first become familiar with. *Productive negative thoughts* are the ones that alert you to genuine threats, motivate necessary change, or inform you about your values and needs. "I feel like crap because I was rude to my sister," or, "The car door needs to be locked so my vintage cassette collection doesn't get stolen."

Unproductive negative thoughts, on the other hand, cause suffering without giving useful guidance. These include ruminating on unchangeable past events, catastrophizing about doomsday future scenarios, or harsh self-criticism that breaks you down rather than building you up. Thoughts like, "I'm a bad person with no hope of improving" or "Nobody will like me if I can't get to places on time" are some clear examples. Note, however, that not all negative thinking needs reframing; the key is distinguishing between thoughts that help you navigate life effectively, and those that create unnecessary distress without offsetting benefits.

When working to make this distinction you'll want to be on the lookout for a few of the most common cognitive distortions I notice from my clients:

Catastrophization. Jumping to the worst possible outcome when faced with the unknown. *"My boss seemed mad today, probably because I messed up big time and now I'm going to get fired and won't be able to afford rent anymore."*

Rumination. A long period of time focused on repetitive and often negative thoughts. *Spending all day replaying an awkward conversation with your crush from last week, analyzing every word said and convincing yourself that you came across as annoying.*

Polarized thinking. Also known as all-or-nothing thinking, this is when you can only identify the extreme ends of a situation or possible outcome. *"I ate a slice of cake even though I'm on a diet, so I've completely failed and might as well give up entirely."*

Mind reading. Guessing what someone else may be thinking and giving those assumed thoughts negative weight. *"My partner is being quiet tonight—they're definitely upset with me about something."*

Mental filtering. Ignoring the positives and paying unbalanced attention to the negatives. *Receiving mostly positive feedback on your comedy performance but hyperfixating on the one suggestion for improvement and letting that one small bad thing sour an otherwise good day.*

Should statements. Self-shaming thoughts around unrealistic expectations, based on past memories or the future. *"I should be further along in my career by now,"* or *"I should have known better than to trust them."*

Magnification. An over-exaggeration of a thought, making it seem like a bigger deal than it is. *Viewing a minor miscommunication as a relationship-ending blunder, or believing that forgetting someone's name is a sign of developing early dementia.*

Minimization. The opposite of the above, ignoring the significance of a thought or situation out of conscious or subconscious avoidance. *Downplaying a genuine accomplishment by saying, "Anyone could have done that."*

Blaming. Assuming that only others are the cause or at fault for any issue. Saying *"I can't succeed because my family doesn't support me,"* while avoiding taking personal responsibility for effort and choices.

The goal of reframing in these instances isn't to eliminate the thought patterns entirely (they're part of being human) but to recognize when they're operating so you can choose whether to believe them or to reframe them.

EXERCISE 13.3 IDENTIFYING YOUR THOUGHT PATTERNS

My most common negative thought loops:
- Catastrophizing
- Rumination
- All-or-nothing thinking
- Mind reading
- Mental filtering
- Should statements
- Magnification
- Minimization
- Blaming

Where this came up most recently:

My automatic thought:

How this made me feel:

How it affected my behavior:

Is this thought productive or unproductive?
- Productive (alerts me to issues, motivates change)
- Unproductive (causes suffering without helpful guidance)

If unproductive, what cognitive distortion is this?

Core Reframing Techniques

The ABCD Method

The *ABCD method* provides a structured approach to reframing derived from Rational Emotive Behavior Therapy and Cognitive Behavioral Therapy (Zaboski et al., 2021). It stands for **A**ctivating event, **B**elief, **C**onsequence, and **D**ispute.

A. First, identify the activating event, or the situation triggering your response. (Your boss just sent you a text that says, "We need to talk tomorrow.")

B. Next, notice your belief or interpretation about the event. (You start to think, "Oh my gosh I'm going to get fired and they won't even give me a chance to wrap up anything I was doing on this project, which means my whole team will suffer and hate me forever. No one will be a reference for me when I have to find my next job.")

C. Then observe the consequence, such as the emotional and behavioral results from that belief. (You realize that your heart rate is now racing just from those thoughts, you feel upset and stressed, and you fall into your typical, possibly self-sabotaging, coping mechanisms for the emotions that have emerged from your interpretation.)

D. Finally, dispute the belief by examining evidence for and against it. (You might instead think, "I recently completed a project that got good feedback from a coworker, and my boss is more likely to review that work than fire me for some unknown reason." Feelings of confidence may emerge, and your body's stress response system can relax.)

For example, if a friend doesn't return your text (A), you might believe they're upset with you (B), leading to anxiety and withdrawal (C). Disputing this thinking might involve recognizing they could be busy, have phone issues, or simply have forgotten to respond (D).

Alternative Explanations

Looking for *alternative explanations* and perspectives is another fundamental reframing skill often used in Cognitive Behavior Therapy. When faced with a situation that triggers negative thoughts, see if you can deliberately generate at least three possible interpretations besides your initial reaction. Using the example from above, if a friend takes longer than usual to respond to your text, rather than assuming they are unhappy with you, consider whether they might be preoccupied with personal matters, tired from poor sleep, or physically separated from their phone as they manage their daily responsibilities. This practice reminds you that your initial interpretation, while feeling compelling, is just one of many possible ways to understand the situation. Over time, this habit creates cognitive flexibility—the ability to shift perspective rather than becoming locked into a single interpretation that may create unnecessary distress.

Evidence Examination

Evidence examination similarly tests negative beliefs against reality rather than taking them at face value. When a difficult thought arises ("I'm not going to be able to get this business off the ground" or "My friend is probably angry with me"), treat it as a hypothesis to be investigated rather than a fact to be believed. Ask yourself: What real-world evidence supports this belief? What evidence contradicts it? Am I confusing feelings with facts? Would I reach the same conclusion if someone else presented this evidence to me?

This approach brings in your rational mind to evaluate emotional thoughts, creating a more balanced assessment (also known as using the Wise Mind in Dialectical Behavioral Therapy, developed by Marsha Linehan and introduced in 1993). It's similar to how a scientist would test a hypothesis through careful examination of evidence rather than through intuition or assumption.

Future-Focused Reframing

Future-focused reframing is a technique that is particularly helpful for all of my anxious people out there. It specifically addresses anticipatory anxiety, which causes worry about events that haven't even happened yet. This approach involves applying the alternative explanations technique through the lens of future forecasting.

Suppose you're anxious about an upcoming social gathering, for example. In that case, your mind might automatically picture tripping over the doorstep on your way in and therefore knocking a precious vase to the floor, then bumping into another guest as you're trying to rescue the vase, and spilling their drink all over the front of their white trousers—all before you've made it into the place. Future reframing involves consciously creating alternative scenarios that range from the experience being somewhat challenging ("I might stumble on an unexpected step or carpet") to surprisingly positive ("I can't wait to celebrate my sister and meet her new friends"), boosted by specific plans for managing various outcomes without indulging in excessive anxiety-based planning. This practice counteracts the tendency to conflate possibility with probability—turning "it could happen" into "it will happen"—and reminds you of your capacity to handle different scenarios, even difficult ones. It's like mentally rehearsing multiple possible scripts rather than fixating on a single worst-case version.

Reframing Self-Talk

Reframing self-talk and internal narratives addresses how you speak to yourself about yourself. Believe it or not, most people have an internal dialogue that's far harsher than anything they would say to a friend facing similar circumstances. To reframe your own internal monologue, notice your habitual self-talk. ("I'm such an idiot; how could I make that mistake?" or "I'll never get better at this.") Then deliberately create more balanced alternatives in your mind. ("That mistake doesn't define my intelligence," or "I'm still learning and improvement takes time,") The goal here isn't to participate in artificially positive self-talk—again, we want to avoid toxic positivity—but rather re-direct your self-criticism to the kind of balanced, supportive perspective you might offer to someone you care about.

Situational Reframing

Daily stressors that can contribute to small but cumulative irritations of everyday life are great candidates for *situational reframing*. Traffic jams become opportunities for audiobook enjoyment (my personal go-to) or mindful breathing. A long line at the store becomes a chance to practice patience, or notice interesting details about your surroundings. Technology glitches become reminders of how much we typically benefit from functioning systems. (But thank goodness the days of dial-up Internet are long gone.) Reframing in this way doesn't mean pretending annoyances are actually pleasant, but rather finding legitimate alternative perspectives that can help reduce unnecessary suffering. Over time, this habit creates remarkable shifts in your day-to-day experience, transforming potential frustrations into neutral or even positive moments.

Meaning-Making

If you want to transform tough experiences, *meaning-making* can help you find purpose or significance in life's much harder challenges. This shifts even the most dreaded situations (losing a job or loved one, being diagnosed with a long-term illness) from experiences of pure suffering to opportunities for growth or connection. Being able to practice this can be the difference between life and death, as Viktor Frankl (1946), who survived Nazi concentration camps, observed that people who could reach to find moments of personal connection and meaning in their oppression were more likely to endure the extreme hardship and survive.

While most of us face less extreme challenges, the principle remains true—finding meaning in difficulty creates resilience. A health crisis could deepen your appreciation for life, or job loss might open a path to more liberating work, just as relationship struggles can teach you important truths about yourself. It's the difference between a painful experience being solely destructive and one that, while still painful, also contains seeds of growth or connection.

EXERCISE 13.4 REFRAMING PRACTICE TOOLKIT

Choose a recent negative thought and work through these techniques.

My negative thought:

ABCD Method.
- **A** (activating event):
- **B** (belief/interpretation):
- **C** (consequence–behavior/emotions):
- **D** (dispute–alternative evidence):

Alternative Explanations:

Evidence Examination:

Evidence *for* my original thought:

Evidence *against* my original thought:
- Am I confusing any feelings with facts?
- Reflection on any other reframe you want to try:
- How does this reframed thought feel different?

Reframing Requires Balance

If you're thinking to yourself, "Okay, I can see how this could be helpful but I'm still not sure if it'll work *for me*," you're not alone. Skepticism about gratitude or reframing often has legitimate origins. Perhaps positive thinking was used to dismiss your valid concerns in the past, or toxic positivity made you feel your authentic emotions were unwelcome. Other resistance might stem from the physical discomfort of building new neural pathways (literally, your brain prefers familiar thought patterns even when they're unhelpful), fear that acknowledging positives might prevent necessary change, or concern that focusing on gratitude minimizes serious problems.

Remember that these practices are not meant to dilute or replace difficult thoughts, emotions, or experiences. Instead, they are designed to expand your attention to include positive aspects of your rich and complex life, alongside the obvious challenges. You're adjusting your mental camera lens to capture a wider shot that includes both shadows and light, rather than zooming in exclusively on either. We want to invite balance to our thoughts, which will hopefully cascade into balance everywhere else in our lives.

EXERCISE 13.5 PERSONAL PRACTICE PLAN

My gratitude commitment.
- Format:
- Frequency:
- Time of day:

My reframing commitment.
- I'll practice reframing when I notice:
- My go-to reframing technique is:
- How I'll remember to use it:

Integration with daily life.
- Situations where I'll practice gratitude:
- Trigger thoughts I'll practice reframing:

Potential obstacles and solutions.
- Obstacle:
- Solution:

How I'll track my progress:
- Mood improvements
- Fewer negative spirals

- Better sleep
- More positive outlook

Signs I might need help:
- I can't find anything to be grateful for (for over two weeks)
- Reframing feels impossible or makes things worse
- My thoughts become extremely negative or hopeless

Chapter 14

Journaling for Self-Expression and Insight

If your mind is a house, journaling would be both the window that lets in fresh air and the broom that helps clear away the cobwebs. The gratitude practices and reframing techniques we explored in the previous chapter give you powerful tools for shifting your mental landscape, and now journaling offers you a literal blank page on which you can explore, develop, and integrate these approaches more deeply. Beyond simply recording daily events, journaling is a powerful tool for self-discovery, emotional processing, and personal growth. It creates a dedicated space where you can have an honest conversation with yourself, free from judgment (from yourself or others) or interruption.

In this chapter, we'll explore the transformative potential of putting pen to paper (or fingers to keyboard or screen). Building on the relaxation techniques, gratitude practices, and reframing skills from previous chapters, journaling offers a way to deepen these methods and integrate them more fully into your life. Whether you're new to journaling or have shelves full of completed notebooks, we'll go over fresh approaches that align with your unique needs and goals.

How Journaling Rewires Your Brain

Journaling works by creating a *bilateral processing* experience, which is a fancy way of saying that the information you're writing about gets processed through both the left and right hemispheres of your brain. While thinking on its own engages certain regions in your brain, the physical act of writing activates additional motor areas and results in elevated engagement. When you write, you're essentially using both the creative, emotional right hemisphere in conjunction with the logical, analytical left hemisphere. This whole-brain activation helps integrate different forms of processing, which may explain why writing often leads to insights that thinking alone doesn't produce. You're looping in both the artistic and engineering departments of your mental organization in a collaborative project.

Additionally, when you're journaling, you're externalizing thoughts on paper or screen, which creates psychological distance that allows you to observe your own thinking more objectively. When thoughts remain in your head, you're more likely to be completely wrapped up in them. Once they're written down, these same thoughts become objects you can examine from different angles.

A healthy detachment from what's going on in your mind lets you take the next step in the process of *neural integration*— building the bridge between the limbic system (your emotional brain) and the prefrontal cortex (your thinking brain). Through this process, you calm your brain's immediate alarm system and bring in an objective "manager" to more effectively sort through your thoughts. This integration helps prevent you from being either emotionally flooded or intellectually detached from your experiences, creating a more balanced internal state that those of us in the field of psychology call the "window of tolerance."

Beyond bilateral integration, regular journaling can also improve cognitive, emotional, and psychosomatic functioning. Journaling helps clear out the mental clutter, so that heightened working memory and cognitive processing can occur. Your brain's working memory—its mental workspace—has limited capacity. When it's clogged up with unprocessed thoughts and emotions, you have less bandwidth available for other cognitive tasks. Journaling helps transfer content from working memory to long-term storage, freeing up your mental resources. Studies show that university students who journal regularly experience improved academic performance, not because the journaling itself involves reviewing academic information, but because it enhances their cognitive efficiency by reducing the background noise (Connor-Greene, 2000).

Enhanced emotional regulation also develops through journaling because doing so helps you navigate feelings without being overwhelmed by them. Individuals who journal frequently become less likely to snap in anger, spiral into anxiety, or sink into sadness. This regulation happens partly because journaling helps you identify emotional patterns earlier, before they reach overwhelming intensity, and partly because journaling strengthens your capacity to experience feelings without immediately reacting to them. In this way, journaling is like developing stronger emotional muscles through regular exercise, allowing you to carry heavier emotional loads without getting hurt.

At this point in the book, you might not be surprised to learn that regular journaling correlates to better sleep quality and reduced stress-related health symptoms. Writing, particularly in the evening, seems to serve as a mental "dump" that prevents rumination when you're laying in bed trying to sleep. Since we know that stress has physical consequences, it makes sense that regular journalers also experience fewer stress-related physical complaints like headaches, digestive issues, and tension. These benefits likely stem from getting "un-stuck" from negative thoughts and the physiological relaxation that often comes with the journaling process.

Journaling Methods

So how the heck do we actually journal? When I check in with my clients about journaling practices they've used prior to therapy, the most common method they've reported using is occasionally creating an emotional release in their notes app. This often occurs when they're feeling heightened emotions and just need an outlet. I think this is a great practice for journaling newbies, which we can elevate by adding in more intentional structure.

But like most things in life, journaling is not a one-size-fits-all activity. If you've thought about journaling in the past but never went forward with it, you might not have found the style of journaling that works best for you yet. Let's cover a few different ways to go about the practice.

Free Writing

Stream-of-consciousness writing means putting your thoughts into words with no structure or method: just recording whatever comes to mind in the order, or disorder, that it naturally comes to you in. The only rule for this style of writing is to keep writing continuously, without censoring, editing, or judging. This approach bypasses your internal critic and gets to the material that might not emerge during more structured reflection. While this might initially produce seemingly random content, you'll find that patterns and insights are likely to emerge over time like puzzle pieces that eventually reveal a coherent image when enough are connected.

Morning Pages

If you want to provide a little more structure and routine to your journaling, *morning pages* are essentially a three-page "brain dump" popularized by Julia Cameron in *The Artist's Way* (1992). The process involves writing three full pages of long-hand, stream-of-consciousness writing first thing in the morning—before you do anything else. These pages aren't meant to be articulate or even re-read regularly. Instead, they serve as a daily mental clearing, a way to download thoughts, worries, and ideas before beginning your day.

Timed Writing

Timed writing can also provide structure to unstructured free writing. Setting a timer, typically for 10 to 20 minutes, can create boundaries that paradoxically enhance freedom of writing and expression. Knowing there's a defined endpoint helps quiet the part of your mind that might question the process or bring up practical concerns like "How long should I keep going?" or "Is this worth my time?" Timing your writing sessions also creates gentle pressure that helps bypass overthinking. (Remember the concept of healthy stress levels from Chapter 11.) When you know you have limited time, you're more likely to write continuously rather than pausing to second-guess yourself. You're likely to find that your writing becomes noticeably more authentic and insightful in the final minutes of a timed session, as initial surface thoughts give way to deeper material.

Journal Prompts

Lastly, using prompts to kick off your free-writing journaling session can help you focus on a particular theme. Prompts can be especially helpful when you're feeling stuck or new to journaling. The best prompts are open-ended enough to allow for personal exploration while specific enough to spark genuine reflection: "What am I pretending not to know?" or "When did I feel most alive this week?" For others, starting with a blank page offers complete freedom but requires more self-direction. Experienced journalers sometimes alternate between these approaches, using prompts when they need focus or inspiration and blank-page writing when they want to discover what emerges without a specific direction.

Structured Reflection Journaling

If you're anything like me, the idea of free writing is stress-inducing enough to want to avoid journaling altogether. Luckily for us, structured writing is an option that provides scaffolding for deep self-exploration. This style helps you examine the multiple layers of your experience while preventing any habit of circling around familiar and unproductive thought patterns. Structured journaling frameworks are like having a skilled interviewer asking you thoughtful questions instead of trying to interview yourself. The structure brings out insights that might not come up through less directed reflection.

Decision-Making Journals

Decision-making journals are great for supporting you through complex choices. Instead of trying to solve difficult decisions entirely in your head, where options can become a confused tangle, decision journaling creates space to explore possibilities more systematically. Effective approaches I suggest to clients include:

- listing pros and cons in order of weighted importance

- exploring future outcomes about potential feelings in response ("How might I feel about this choice in one month? One year? Five years?")

- examining experiences, thoughts, and emotions in their alignment with your core values

With this method, the journal becomes a laboratory for examining options from multiple angles without the pressure of immediate conclusion or action and often revealing possibilities that weren't initially apparent.

WWW&W

Just like gratitude practices, "what went well and why" reflections can also reinforce positive experiences and build on successes. This practice, created by Martin Seligman and based on his positive psychology research, involves writing about three things that went well during your day and, crucially, exploring why they happened (2012). This "why" component is essential because it helps you identify the conditions, choices, and actions that contributed to positive outcomes, making it more likely you can recreate them.

WOOP

The WOOP method is a simple, to-the-point journaling technique that is quick and effective. Start with a specific **W**ish that's on your mind. Write down this wish, and then zone in on the specific **O**utcome you're wanting, and pinpoint any **O**bstacles that are currently keeping you from reaching that outcome. Then it's time to come up with a **P**lan to reach your goal, or wish. The best part of journaling techniques like the WOOP method is that you can get pretty efficient at it, taking just 5 to 10 minutes of your day to focus on your journaling practice.

Emotional Processing Journaling

If you want to use journaling as a container for intense emotions, consider using an *emotional processing method* for journaling. These approaches are effective because they create boundaries in emotional processing, rather than letting emotions stay as overwhelming internal states. When strong feelings like anger, grief, or anxiety arise, the journal page offers a place to express them in their full intensity without real-world consequences (compared to if your emotions lead to snapping at others or smashing furniture). This containment on its own helps regulate emotions that might otherwise feel unmanageable. Clients have reported that simply knowing this outlet is available—similar to anticipating an upcoming therapy session—helps them navigate difficult feelings more effectively, even when they're not actively writing.

The Unsent Letter

I'm also a fan of the *unsent letter technique*, which allows you to express your thoughts and emotions to another person without directly interacting with them. Write as if addressing someone specifically, and express your complete, unfiltered thoughts and feelings without concern for how they might receive them—and keep in mind they won't even see it unless you decide to share it (or parts of it) with them later. This practice helps process emotions that might be unhelpful to express directly, such as residual anger toward someone in a situation that you've otherwise reconciled, complex feelings about someone who has died, or thoughts you need to clarify for yourself before deciding whether or how to communicate them. It empowers you to understand your emotional response in a safe manner that doesn't impact your relationship just yet.

Dialoguing

Dialoguing is a technique that helps you understand and speak to the different parts of yourself. (For more on this, I recommend looking into the Internal Family Systems therapeutic modality, created by Dr. Richard Schwartz in 2000.) Begin by writing from your current primary perspective, then allow another personified aspect of your experience to respond on the page. This could be your fear, your self-critic, inner teen, or your wiser self. Continue writing out this conversation between the different parts of yourself, switching perspectives with each entry. This practice helps integrate conflicting aspects of your experience and can lead to surprising insights as you access thoughts that are difficult to fully understand on their own. It's particularly valuable when you feel torn between different viewpoints, or when an emotion doesn't make sense but keeps coming up despite your attempts to dismiss it.

Emotional Tracking

If you want to combine logic with emotion, you might enjoy tracking your emotional patterns and triggers in a journal. Over time, tracking your emotions reveals valuable information about how you navigate various situations. A simple approach is to record your different emotional states throughout the day, along with the situations that preceded them. Over weeks or months, review these entries and look for patterns. You might find that certain environments, interactions, or even physical states (hunger, fatigue) consistently lead to specific emotional responses. I've had clients even create spreadsheets to keep track of these emotional patterns, which is actually quite helpful for interpreting data.

VOMIT

I saved my personal favorite journaling structure for last—the *VOMIT system* developed by YouTuber Campbell Walker. The eye-catching name is thankfully an acronym, standing for the different sections that should be utilized in each journaling session: **V**ent, **O**bligations, **M**indset, **I**deate, and **T**rajectory.

At the start of the journaling session, you'll "Vent" and get out all the thoughts and emotions that are causing blockages in your mind. Next, you'll note down any responsibilities or Obligations that can be singled out from the venting. Then you'll check in on your Mindset and see if any thoughts or beliefs can be reframed to contribute to a more growth-oriented or productive mindset. After that comes Ideation, during which you'll brainstorm and create a list of ideas around your goals or to-do items. Lastly, you'll analyze your current Trajectory toward your goals, figuring out the roadblocks, and making any adjustments necessary to keep moving forward.

Finding Your Journaling Style

As you were reading through the different ways to journal, was there any style or specific method that sparked your interest? I'd recommend trusting your gut and trying that way of journaling first. If you're still unsure, that's okay too. Review the list again, taking into consideration your personal way of thinking and even how you prepare for information processing at work or school. If you thrive with clear guidelines and specific outcomes, structured journaling with consistent prompts or systems will likely feel most satisfying and productive. If you value exploration and spontaneity, more freeform approaches like stream-of-consciousness writing or open-ended reflection might better suit your style. If emotional reactions are taking too much space in your life, test out the emotional processing methods.

The best part is, you aren't confined to the techniques that I've listed out here. There are unlimited ways to journal, so feel free to research methods online or combine writing processes that we've talked about in a way that is customized to your needs and preferences.

Just as your journaling practice may vary, your ideal medium may be different, too. I always recommend that clients start with physical, handwritten journaling, as some research suggests that writing by hand engages neural pathways that support learning and memory differently than typing does (Marano et al., 2025). (This is why so many teachers and professors encourage hand-writing notes in class instead of typing on the computer.) Pen-to-paper journaling also provides a sensory experience that feels more contemplative, eliminates screen-related distractions, and creates a tangible record that exists independently of technology. However, digital journaling has its perks, too—offering searchability, privacy (through password protection), accessibility across devices, and often includes helpful features like tags, templates, and reminders.

When it comes to actually sitting down to journal, writing frequency and duration should be compatible with your life circumstances and goals. Consider what rhythm actually fits into your life. A few minutes daily, integrated with your morning coffee routine? A longer weekly session during downtime on your Sunday evening? Occasional but intensive weekend writing retreats? You're going to get sick of me saying this, but I'll keep bringing it up because it's critical to success with habits: the most effective journaling practice is one you'll actually maintain. So align your expectations with your reality rather than imagining you "should" write daily if your life doesn't currently support that pattern.

Overcoming Obstacles

"But I don't know what to write about." I hear this a lot, but I've found that feeling often stems from overthinking or perfectionism rather than actual lack of material. If you're not already using a timed method of journaling, try setting a timer for five minutes and free-write continuously about literally anything, without lifting your pen or judging the content. Dabble with prompts, or simply list out recent thoughts or emotions without diving into them just yet. Remember that seemingly mundane topics often lead to unexpected depth once you begin exploring them on the page.

Similarly, the argument, "I don't have time" sometimes reflects a legitimate concern in busy lives, but dismissively overlooks the power and efficiency of brief, focused writing. You can truly benefit from sessions as short as 5 to 15 minutes, if done consistently. Put away the idea that journaling requires extensive time commitments, and consider micro-journaling approaches. A single question answered thoughtfully in the moments before your lunch break is over, or recording reflections by voice during your commute, can be transformative. These small but regular touchpoints with your inner experience can even yield more impact and change than sporadic longer sessions, just as brief daily tune-in practice are more effective than occasional hour-long sits.

Another common obstacle I hear is "I'm not a good writer," which confuses journaling with performance or publication. (It also speaks to the influence of your inner critic.) Effective journaling doesn't have to be beautiful enough to nominate you for writing awards, nor does it require perfect grammar—only honesty with yourself. The page doesn't judge your writing quality, and unless you choose to share it, neither will anyone else. If this is a prominent concern that persists, experiment with alternative approaches like voice recording, bullet-point writing, or drawing instead of writing. If you're able to push through the initial hesitation, it's likely that writing quality concerns will diminish naturally over time as the benefits of journaling start coming through. Journaling is for your self-discovery and growth, not a writing sample to be critiqued by others.

Using Your Journal As Your Companion

Journaling is one of the most accessible yet underutilized tools available for personal growth and emotional well-being. Unlike many other practices, it requires no special equipment, expertise, or financial investment—just your willingness to show up on the page with honesty and curiosity. The simple act of externalizing your thoughts creates new possibilities for insight, integration, and intentional living that thinking alone rarely provides.

As you develop your journaling practice, remember that there is no "right way" to journal. The most effective approach is the one that resonates with you and that you'll actually maintain over time. Feel free to experiment with different techniques, tweak them to your style and needs, and create your own unique approach to written reflection. Your journal is ultimately a conversation with yourself, and like any good conversation, it should feel natural, engaging, and worthwhile.

Treat your journal as a trusted companion on your journey; it listens without judgment, helps you process your experiences, and reflects back to you your own wisdom and growth. Whether you write daily, weekly, or only during significant life transitions, the page is always there and ready to receive whatever you bring to it. The insights you discover through consistent reflection will complement and deepen the stress management, gratitude, and reframing practices you've already developed, creating an integrated approach to navigating life's complexities with greater clarity and purpose.

Chapter 15

Identifying Your Therapy Goals

Even if you already know what you want to address in therapy, I've often found that what we end up working on in sessions may expand beyond your initial complaint (also known as the *presenting problem* in "therapy speak"). Sometimes couples that come in for intimacy troubles, for example, end up focusing on stress management. Perhaps an individual who wants to address anger outbursts moves to working through unresolved grief. I have two theories so far as to why this "presenting problem switch-up" occurs.

The first is that we're not always fully comfortable diving into our deep, dark secrets and vulnerabilities with strangers—and often with good reason. I mean, how often do we run into someone new and think "Ah, yes, this looks like a good person to tell my childhood fears to?" For most of us, we tend to guard the less-than-perfect parts of ourselves, rather than advertise them, at the onset of a new, interpersonal relationship.

Our instinct is to keep certain walls in place when we meet someone new and only let our guard down as we interpret how emotionally safe that person is as we grow more acquainted. Keeping walls up as a protective measure is relatively healthy in the process of making new acquaintances. Opening up too soon to the wrong person could lead to hurt, especially if the other person hasn't earned that trust through their words and actions. Trying to exempt therapy from this natural protective reflex would be a tricky task. It'd be like changing ingredients in the staple family recipe that you cook on a weekly basis—it hasn't been practiced or proven as the same process you have done in every kitchen session prior.

My second theory about why presenting problems changes through therapy is that, while you might know something is off, you pin the negative symptom on the easiest factor to determine, rather than the deeper, underlying issue.

This would look like being tired all the time because you stay up until 3 a.m. every morning. The in-your-face answer to this is that your sleep routine could be improved. So you decide to see a therapist to work on your habits around sleep, but after a few sessions, you and your therapist begin to see that you're actually surviving your day-to-day life with an overworked nervous system as the result of your demanding career. You stay up way past your bedtime enjoying engaging or relaxing activities, taking the time to calm down your body and your mind. Now the therapy treatment plan shifts from sleep hygiene to focusing on the clarified presenting problem of coping with career demands and preventing the need of late-night nervous system regulation.

If you've been reading this book chapter by chapter, you won't be surprised to hear that there is no perfect way to approach goals for therapy. It is natural for goals to shift and be fluid throughout the therapeutic process. But there are a few areas we can assess together ahead of time to get your wheels turning when it comes to thinking about that initial goal for therapy.

Have You Asked the Magic Question?

With the insight you've gained thus far, let's narrow down what may be your initial presenting problem, and build a few corresponding *therapeutic goals*. Therapeutic goals are the cornerstone of your treatment plan and help to measure progress in therapy. My favorite exercise in working toward identifying these goals is to ask the *magic question*: if I could wave a magic wand over your life and everything would be great, all your problems erased, what would that version of your life look like? If you're rolling your eyes at this technique, you wouldn't be the first. Many of my favorite therapeutic techniques are seemingly goofy on the outside, but true gems that get to the heart of the problem.

Answering the magic question with a straightforward, reality-confined sentence or two will be tempting. But I invite you, just as I do with my clients, to think bigger and outside the box after you come up with the first draft of your response. If an obvious answer comes to you, fill in the details. If you think, "My life would be better if I wasn't sad all the time," what would that look like for you on a daily basis? What is sadness currently preventing you from doing? How would other emotions like contentment, excitement, fear, or hope impact the small details of your day?

You can even add in details that feel frivolous in the moment. Maybe a purple beta fish in a Harry Potter-themed fish bowl makes it into your musings, or perhaps you'd be able to eat ice cream for breakfast every day in your ideal world. These details can add important clues to your hidden wants and needs, despite feeling a little silly while brainstorming.

Let's say that the magically improved version of your life involves being retired and playing basketball every day. That could be a sign that you feel caged in your current daily tasks or job and are lacking in carving out time doing a fulfilling personal hobby or activity. Or maybe you crave a consistent daily routine. Did the magic question get you thinking about moving to a cottage and taking care of farm animals? Take a look at your current environment and see what's keeping you from feeling the comfort and freedom that you would feel in your magic solution. Once you find the key factors, you'll be able to take baby steps toward merging your reality and our magically improved daydream.

EXERCISE 15.1 YOUR MAGIC QUESTION

If we could wave a magic wand over your life to "fix" it, what would look different?

What is Your Motivation?

Another technique that many therapists use at the start of the therapeutic relationship is called *motivational interviewing*. Through motivational interviewing, the therapist collaborates with their client to tease out the differences between the client's current reality and where they want to be. Motivational interviewing takes the magic question a step further by incorporating the client's hopes, wishes, values, needs, and strengths.

For now, take some time to think about the improved version of your life that you are longing for. How does this version meet your needs? Which values do you hold that align with your possible improved self? And what strengths do you have that can help get you there? It may also be worth your time to evaluate values and needs that are not currently being met. Are you neglecting any needs or feeling out of alignment in any values?

Let's say, hypothetically, that you're someone who feels constantly overwhelmed and exhausted, struggling to keep up with work and personal responsibilities. You might discover through a brief self-assessment of your motivations that your core values include creativity and meaningful connection with others. However, your current reality looks like having a demanding job that leaves no time for creative pursuits or time to invest in furthering your relationships with others. You may also realize that your strengths lie in being highly organized and empathetic. The improved version of your life could involve finding work that incorporates your creative talents, having better boundaries to support time for relationships, and using your organizational skills to balance your schedule and responsibilities. In this example, being able to highlight what's important to you can create a clear path to a life that honors the best parts of you.

Pay attention to any patterns that show up as you work through these exercises or reflect on what truly motivates you. You might start noticing connections between your daily struggles and deeper issues around self-worth, communication patterns, or feeling stuck between competing values. Consider the bigger picture factors that might be influencing your situation, which could look like family expectations, cultural pressures, work environment, or even societal messages about things we're told we should care about. If anything pops in your mind, I'd encourage you to write it down and see if any patterns emerge.

Would You Rather be SMART or NICE?

Knowing your goals ahead of therapy can help you and your therapist craft an effective treatment plan from the very beginning. However, there are two different approaches to goal-setting that can significantly impact your motivation and success, so exploring these frameworks first may help you determine which approach resonates most with your personality and circumstances. Taking the time to chart out your goals on paper, rather than keeping mental tabs on them, will make the path to your improved self feel much less daunting when it's separated into digestible, bite-sized chunks.

First let's distinguish between SMART goals and NICE goals, the former being the standard practice and the latter being the new kid on the goal-setting block. SMART goal setting is the classic framework that stands for **S**pecific, **M**easurable, **A**chievable, **R**elevant, and **T**ime-bound goals. Each of these categories helps you move from a single, vague goal to a clearly visualized one that includes actionable steps you can take to reach it. For example, the overall goal of "becoming more active" can be overwhelming and intimidating. Let's break it down into the SMART goal format:

"I will gain three pounds of muscle over the next four months by weight lifting three times a week and eating 100 grams of protein daily."

Specific: gaining three pounds of muscle

Measurable: eating 100 grams of protein a day and tracking weights

Achievable: working out at least three times a week

Relevant: the above support physical activity and fitness

Time-Bound: deadline of four months

To familiarize yourself with this type of goal setting, try breaking one of yours down in this way here:

EXERCISE 15.2 S.M.A.R.T. GOAL

Specific:
Measurable:
Achievable:
Relevant:
Time-Bound:

The newer, NICE goal framework has recently been introduced by Ali Abdaal, author of *Feel Good Productivity* (2023) and part-time critic of SMART goals. This framework incorporates **N**ear-term, **I**nput-based, **C**ontrollable, and **E**nergizing factors. What's unique about the NICE goal framework is that motivation is incorporated. Ali has expressed through his work that a downside of SMART goals is that the main motivation is to simply meet the goal. So you're either not content while the goal is unmet, or briefly content once the goal is met, and are then thrown back into discontent as you move towards the next goal.

If we return to the "becoming more active" example, approaching that goal from the NICE framework may look like this:

"This week, I will move my body through enjoyable exercise for at least 40 minutes a day, four days out of the next seven."

Near-term: Focusing only on this upcoming week

Input-based: Paying attention to the 40-minute time commitment instead of the outcome

Controllable: Committing to a do-able schedule

Energizing: Prioritizing types of exercise that bring joy

To familiarize yourself with this type of goal setting, try breaking one of yours down in this way here:

EXERCISE 15.3 N.I.C.E. GOAL

Near-term:

Input-based:

Controllable:

Energizing:

No matter which framework you decide to move forward with, it's important to materialize it through a written plan. I'm personally partial to handwritten plans because the brain processes physical writing differently than typed notes (See Chapter 14), but either will work. In general, think of this plan as a staircase going from where you are now to where you want to be. Each stair is a smaller step on the path of accomplishing the larger vision. And don't worry, you don't have to take each step on your own. You can recruit support people and enlist your therapist to keep you accountable and help you each step of the way.

Is Fear Blocking Your Goals?

Now here's a question that might really throw you through a loop: if you meet all your goals and step into a version of your life that mirrors the one you dreamed up with the miracle question, would there be any downsides? Sometimes our brains can be quite rude in preferring the current misery that we're familiar with over new, unknown potential misery. There can be an odd comfort in at least knowing what to expect in the current situation you're in, even if you're unhappy with it.

Common reflections my clients share when I ask this question is fear of relapsing after tasting the comfort of improvement. There is something so scary about the imagined backslide into discomfort that makes us hesitant to attempt lifting out of our current discomfort in the first place.

This fear is particularly common in clients who have experienced a setback in the past. Maybe they have overcome depression before only to find themselves struggling again months later, or they've successfully managed anxiety for a period before it returned with a vengeance. This fear can be so powerful that people unconsciously sabotage their own progress—stopping therapy right when it's working, abandoning healthy habits just as they're becoming routine, or picking fights with supportive people in their lives. Understanding this pattern is crucial because once you recognize it, you can work with your therapist to develop strategies for navigating the natural ups and downs of recovery without abandoning the journey entirely.

Perhaps you might be afraid of the next steps after reaching your goal. If you want to be successful in your career, for example, the mental burden of anticipating how to maintain that success once you gain the promotion you've been striving for may block your motivation to attempt leveling up in the first place. These anticipated "cons" aren't always logical, but they are understandable. Try out a reframe approach from the previous chapter, such as: *success will likely challenge you in new and unexpected ways, and those challenges will push you to continue growing and building your skills.*

Fear is like a villain in a scary movie. It starts out as a vague idea creeping around the fringes: a subliminal threat. You first notice the signs—faint tapping on the windows or a door left ajar—and your brain kicks into gear in imagining the worst scenarios possible. Is it a vampire, a ghost, a giant spider, or a beast unknown? Your actions then start responding to the imagined threat. You keep a night-light on and add locks to the door that leads to the basement. You're constantly on edge in anticipation until one day you're forced to confront it, or it confronts you.

The reveal of the villain is a make-or-break situation in scary movies. Film producers know that the more mystical and illusive, the scarier it is. But oftentimes, the revealed antagonist can actually make the movie flop. All of a sudden, you get a glimpse of the Babadook that's been played up so largely in the story, and you think, "Eh, the CGI on that is actually pretty lame." Suddenly, your fear starts to plateau.

We are similarly impacted off the silver screen. We often wade through unrealized fears that are impacting our choices and actions throughout the day, even if we're not consciously analyzing them. But once we're able to unmask the root fear (I imagine in a very Scooby-Doo-like style), we often see it's manageable and perhaps even a little silly.

Still, fear is one of the biggest roadblocks to pursuing goals, and contributes greatly to self-sabotage. So it may be worth thinking through the fears you're holding, as you reflect on your goals, in order to address them in partnership with your therapist and move past any blocks.

EXERCISE 15.4 UNBLOCK FEAR

List three fears that might be holding you back.

How Do Therapists Use Goals in Therapy?

This may or may not be an industry secret, but therapists typically have goals in mind for each client's treatment progress, in addition to those set by the clients themselves. Although your therapist doesn't have a series of boxes you need to check during your work together, they do often set goals to measure your progress together.

This is because therapists have different approaches to *treatment planning*, a.k.a. the literal formulation of their plan for your path in therapy. Many therapists write out this plan, including your symptoms, goals in improving or reducing these symptoms, methods to reach those goals, and signs to anticipate when you might be ready to end treatment. Some therapists are collaborative with their clients in treatment planning, and others stick to clinical protocols, like therapists who must provide standardized notes and treatment plans to insurance companies or psychologists who have rigid diagnostic procedures. Don't be afraid to ask to be clued in if you'd like to be part of treatment planning! Going over each of the sections of a treatment plan can make for a really interesting and productive therapy session, and as a bonus, can have you looking forward to your future therapeutic progress.

So what formula do therapists use for making the treatment plan goals? The easiest way to sum it up is that we look for things that we either want to ramp up or ramp down. In clinical terms, treatment goals usually include the verbiage "increase" and "decrease" in conjunction with certain signs or symptoms. If we circle back to the sleep example from the start of this chapter (which is something that impacts almost all of us at some point in time), basic treatment plan would say that we'd want to work towards increased frequency of practicing sleep hygiene, increased use of nervous system regulating tools, and decreased levels of reported stress.

What Are Realistic Expectations?

As with most things in the world of therapy, there typically is flexibility in terms of how goals show up in sessions and in overall treatment. If the goals are no longer applicable due to changing life circumstances or shifting treatment plans, then we alter the therapy goals appropriately. We can also make new goals if you conquer the first ones. Or, as I often see in my practice, is that we bounce between goals that become more relevant as life circumstances shift. A college student originally worried about fitting in could shift their goals to managing academic stress if he came to grow a great group of friends. A couple struggling with infertility might move to new financial stresses if they come to acceptance and appreciation of a child-free future.

The beauty of life is that it is ever-evolving. We are ever-evolving. And thus, therapy will be ever-evolving.

Self-Compassion in Goal Setting

Identifying a goal may sound easy on paper, but the process of solidifying your goal can be both an art and science balancing the requirements of honest self-reflection and flexibility to evolve as you grow and change. The information and exercises in this chapter aren't meant to lock you into rigid expectations but rather to help you approach therapy with greater self-awareness and intentionality. Whether you discovered that your initial presenting problem might be covering up deeper issues, or that sneaky fears are subtly sabotaging your progress, doing this preparation work and exploration gives you valuable material to bring into your therapy space.

Keep in mind that therapy goals aren't set in stone. I frequently remind the individuals I work with that progress can blossom when both the therapist and client remain open to adjusting course as new insights emerge. Your therapist brings clinical knowledge and objective perspective while you bring the intimate expertise that you have in understanding yourself. Your ability to delve into new areas of self-understanding is bound to produce meaningful therapeutic outcomes.

As you move toward finding and beginning work with a therapist, carry with you the understanding that goal-setting in therapy is an ongoing process. The clarity you've gained in this chapter will serve as a valuable starting point, but be prepared for your goals to deepen, shift, or expand as you develop greater insight into yourself. Flexibility isn't a sign of confusion or failure, but rather a natural part of growth and a signal of your willingness to remain curious about yourself.

Chapter 16

Finding the Right Therapist

If you've been following through the previous chapters up to this point, you've likely gathered some clues about what you want to work on in therapy. Now it's time for a critical step—finding the right therapist to work *with*.

Therapy Modalities

Here's a tip that I learned from my own trial and error of finding therapists in the past: it is super beneficial to first analyze what type of therapy you'd be most comfortable with. *Therapy modality* is the term used to distinguish different types of therapy from one another. If you're not familiar with the different types, I like to break them down into three different buckets: talk therapies, interactive therapies, and active therapies.

The main distinguishing factors between these three categories are the ratio of how much you're talking as compared to how much your therapist may talk, and how much work you have to put in both during sessions and outside of sessions.

As you read through the following modalities, check in with your gut reaction. Some people thrive with structured approaches that provide clear exercises and homework, while others prefer a more open-ended, exploratory process. Neither is better or worse. They're just different paths to the same destination of feeling better.

Talk Therapy Modalities

Traditional talk therapy is probably what most people envision when thinking about therapy—you talk for most of the session while your therapist listens and chimes in every once in a while with a question or thought. These are some of the therapy modalities that fit into this category:

Psychoanalysis. Uses free association (a clinical term for word vomiting) to explore the unconscious

Psychodynamic. Digging into the unconscious through discussion

Humanistic & Person-Centered. Self-exploration with the guidance of a therapist

Narrative. Understanding your own personal narrative and how to reframe your life stories

Existential. Investigating meaning and purpose in life, and understanding experiences through this investigation

Interactive Therapy Modalities

If you'd prefer to have some more back-and-forth with your therapist, and maybe even practice skills and tools in sessions, then interactive modalities might be a better fit for you. These are more structured than talk therapies, but still allow for exploration:

Internal Family Systems (IFS). Getting to know and engage the different "parts" of you through discussion and exercises

Motivational Interviewing (MI). Structured conversation with a therapist to bolster motivation and commitment to change within areas of your life

Eye Movement Desensitization and Reprocessing (EMDR). Using bilateral stimulation (usually a moving light to follow with your eyes) while recalling emotional memories from your past

Brainspotting. Utilizing a visual tool to locate a memory in your brain and bring it forward for targeted processing

Somatic Experiencing (SE). Focusing on bodily awareness and practicing physical exercises to understand and regulate emotional responses

Art Therapy. Processing emotions and thoughts during therapy sessions through various art mediums and creative exercises

Active Therapy Modalities

If physical practice sounds perfect for you, you'd be on the right track with an active modality. Not only are you putting in the work during sessions, but you're likely to get homework to practice between sessions, too. These therapies are the most structured of the three categories and typically involve significant learning and practice both in and outside of sessions:

Cognitive Behavioral Therapy (CBT): Identifies and reframes negative thought patterns

Dialectical Behavior Therapy (DBT). Incorporates skills practice in mindfulness, distress tolerance, and emotional regulation

Exposure Therapy (including ERP for OCD). Involves challenging fears both in-session and structured homework

Acceptance and Commitment Therapy (ACT). Uses mindfulness, cognitive defusion, and commitment to action

Mindfulness-Based Stress Reduction (MBSR). Implementing regular mindfulness practice both inside and outside of therapy sessions

Neurofeedback. Provides brainwave response feedback in session with training to continue at home

What Type of Professional Do You Want to Work With?

I've been using the term *therapist* throughout this book, but there are actually many different types of professionals who are able to conduct therapy sessions or provide therapeutic treatments. Let's understand the different types of professionals in the easiest way I can categorize them for you: how many years of school and training they needed to enter into their professional role.

Coaches

This first category admittedly can't provide clinical therapy at all (legally, at least), but they do sometimes get trained on and practice certain therapeutic-adjacent techniques. There's a coach for nearly every issue you may face, from mental health coaches, trauma coaches, life coaches, career coaches, and more. There are even specialized coaches like ADHD coaches and mindfulness coaches. I once had a client tell me about a coach she found who specialized in helping people find love!

Coaches may see clients one-on-one, and often run coaching groups with multiple participants. I view coaching as a tool that is most useful in elevating you to where you want to be, as sessions are often more future-facing than looking into your past.

My only caveat about coaching options is that this is an unregulated field. For example, unlike the remaining types of providers we'll cover, there's no universal way to report a coach who is acting unethically or even harmfully. Pricing is also unregulated, so fees may range from very affordable to an almost exploitative price tag. For example, I've seen coaching groups that are over $10,000 per participant. This lack of regulation is why insurance companies avoid covering coaching sessions and instead lean toward legally qualified therapy service providers.

If you are more comfortable with the idea of working with a coach, I'd suggest doing your research and getting referrals from people you know and trust. While there can be unqualified people offering coaching service—because anyone can adopt the professional title of "coach" without any training or certifications—there are a plethora of qualified professionals who are expert coaches. Also, if paying a higher fee for services makes you more invested in committing to your personal growth, then you have found your own best answer!

Psychotherapists

There are many different types of degrees and licensure that can qualify someone to provide psychotherapy. A baseline requirement in the United States is typically a Master's degree in Counseling, Marriage and Family Therapy, or Social Work.

However, individuals with PhDs and PsyDs may also qualify to become psychotherapists. After completing their education, these professionals must engage in supervised work until they qualify for their state's licensure requirements and pass a licensing exam.

As you begin to look at psychotherapist titles, you may start to notice quite a bit of "alphabet soup," the term my professors often used in reference to the professional qualification abbreviations after a provider's name. But these letters are simply there to indicate the particular expertise each therapist has.

Individuals who are still under supervision, for example, often have an *A* (for associate) at the start of the initials after their name, or even the word *intern*. Providers who completed their qualifications should have an *L* (for licensed) at the start. The remaining letters should indicate what type of degree that individual attained, like *MFT* for Marriage and Family Therapy or *SW* for Social Work. You should be able to find information on their license standing on your state's licensure website to see if their license is up-to-date or if it has ever been revoked for disciplinary reasons. (For example, I'm working as a Marriage and Family Therapist for now, and hoping to see clients as a PhD one day.)

Psychotherapists can work with clients one-on-one or in groups, similar to coaches. While they are not qualified to prescribe medication, psychotherapists do use treatment plans in working with clients and can consult with your medication prescriber to collaborate on treatment if needed. Psychotherapists are able to assess for and provide diagnoses for disorders that are listed in the Diagnostic and Statistical Manual of Mental Disorders (DSM), but they are not able to do extensive psychological testing to the level that psychologists can.

Psychologists

To become a psychologist, one has to complete a PhD or PsyD, gain supervised hours of providing services, and pass a licensure exam. Psychologists cannot prescribe medications, but they are able to do in-depth psychological evaluations.

These are the professionals you'd look for if you need an assessment done for legal or educational institutions. Psychologists are commonly sought out for ADHD, autism, and learning disorder assessments that can help pave the way to necessary accommodations. You can also find psychologists in non-psychotherapy roles in hospital or government positions, and even in academia and research fields.

Psychiatrists

Finally we get to the professions who can prescribe medicine along with practicing therapy: psychiatrists, psychiatric physicians assistants (PAs), and psychiatric mental health nurse practitioners (PMHNPs). I wanted to highlight PAs and PMHNPs because they are often overlooked, or not even known about, in the field of psychiatry. These are professionals who have completed specialized training in a Master's program focusing on psychiatric care. The great part about working with PAs and PMHNPs is that they are qualified professionals who can provide psychotherapy and medication management at a lower cost than psychiatrists.

Psychiatrists are the most educated professionals on this list, which means there is also a longer list of services they're able to provide. Psychiatrists are able to work with patients for psychotherapy, medication management, and assessments. That said, not all psychiatrists do it all. Some might prefer only medication management and refer you to another professional for psychotherapy, and others might prefer sticking with assessments.

How to *Literally* Find a Therapist

If you have more clarity over what type of provider and modality you're interested in working with, it's time to check out the roster and narrow down a shortlist of professionals who might be a good fit. Whatever you're searching for, keep in mind to look for a therapist who practices in the state that you live in, even if you want to do virtual sessions, because therapists are legally only able to offer therapy services in the state in which they are licensed.

Once you're ready, the two main ways you can go about finding potential therapists are through directories and referrals.

Directories

A quick online search will pull up pages and pages of potential directories for finding your future therapist. Online directories typically list the provider's name and qualifications, a general idea of their fees, the symptoms they specialize in or the therapeutic modalities they use, their location, and whether or not they do virtual sessions. Some provider profiles will indicate whether a certain therapist is currently accepting new clients, but keep in mind that availability is not always accurately updated all the time. When you're deciding which directory to use, the three main types you're likely to come across are:

> **General online directories.** Websites like Psychology Today and TherapyDen are comprehensive and allow you to narrow down your search by specialty, demographics

of the provider, and more. Therapists can customize their own pages and you can typically message them with an inquiry through the site directly, or through the contact information listed on their profile.

Specific directories. Usually focusing on demographics or symptom focus, these directories can help you hone in on specific types of practice. These include faith-based providers in your area, LGBTQIA+ community-focused therapists, grief-specific services, and more.

Insurance directories. Most insurance companies have a patient portal that includes a directory search for providers they cover. If you want to go through your insurance and avoid private-pay fees, this is the most effective route to ensuring that the therapists you find will be in-network.

Referrals

Referrals are clinicians who have been personally or professionally recommended by someone you know. The great thing about referrals is that you can receive a customized shortlist of potential therapists from someone who understands who you are, and which therapist might work well with you. Here are a couple people you might find yourself receiving referrals from:

Doctor referral. Similar to insurance directories, getting a referral from your doctor is helpful if you want to look for in-network providers. Depending on the issue for which you're being referred, your doctor might be able to narrow down a therapist who specializes in the problem area you want to address. Keep in mind, however, that not all referrals from doctors are custom-created for each patient.

Current therapist referral. This may come to you as a surprise, but it's okay to ask for or receive a referral from your current therapist. If you're already seeing a therapist and it's not working for you, they too may likely understand where the conflict is, and could refer you to a colleague whom would be a better fit.

Friend or family referral. There are some pros and cons to weigh when it comes to receiving referrals from friends or family. The biggest pro is that your friends and family know you well and are able to give you insight on the therapist they're recommending. They want to set you up for success because they care about you. However, if the therapist is someone who is already working with that friend or family member, there are two small cons to consider. First, some therapists prefer to not work with friends or family members of current clients in order to remain objective and prevent any conflicts of interest. Secondly, you or your referring loved one may feel anxious about confidentiality if you want to talk about each other in your individual sessions. Though therapists are ethically bound to keep confidentiality, your feelings about this are important to consider.

Options for Therapy Costs

One of the biggest roadblocks we encounter in this process is the affordability of therapy. Prices of everything are rising each year, including session fees. It can be frustrating to find a therapist whom you would love to work with, only to find out that they charge above your budget for services. If you have a specific cost limit, there are a few options available to you:

Sliding-scale. If paying a full fee is not possible for you, then it may be worth seeking a therapist who provides sliding-scale or reduced-fee. Sliding-scale fees are adjusted according to your income. There can be ethical and legal requirements in almost every state when it comes to determining a sliding-scale fee, so don't be surprised if the therapist or administrator asks to see your W-2, recent pay stubs, and/or a standardized form to determine affordability.

Reduced-fee. Similar to sliding-scale, the reduced-fee option is for individuals whose income is below the average threshold set by the therapist, group, or agency. These are typically fixed fees, so they're not customized to each income—unlike sliding-scale fees.

Pro bono. Some therapists keep spots open for clients who need their fee entirely waived. Be prepared to send over financial information so that the therapist or administrator can evaluate qualification for this type of pro-bono work. There may also be an established timetable for discounted services, as well as a regular re-evaluation period. So for example, in three or six months you may be required to re-submit updated financial information to continue to qualify for the fee reduction or pro bono services.

Insurance. If you are insured and would like to see a therapist who is in-network, you will likely pay a co-pay toward your therapist's fee, and your insurance company will pay the rest. Because each person's insurance coverage varies, it's best to check your policy or call a representative from your insurance company to understand what fees for therapy may look like for in-network providers.

Superbill reimbursement. When you meet with a therapist who is not in-network with your insurance company, but you would like to be reimbursed by your insurance, you can try superbill reimbursement. Your therapist gives you a specific type of receipt for your therapy sessions (or super-bill), which you send to your insurance company. The insurer then decides what percentage of the cost, if any, they can reimburse you for.

Request a Consultation

Once you've settled on a few therapists you're interested in, I'd recommend setting up a quick consultation call with them if possible. It's common for therapists to offer a 10- to 20-minute free consultation to help you both determine if you're a good therapeutic fit for one another.

A consultation call allows you to evaluate their approach, communication style, and whether you feel comfortable being vulnerable with them. (Or: if you "vibe" with them.) Statistically, the "vibe" is one of the bigger determining factors in whether or not therapy will be effective for you with this therapist, because if you don't feel comfortable with them, you won't see as much progress in therapy. An added bonus to a free consultation is that you can avoid paying an initial session fee if it's not a good fit prior to that first appointment.

What should you talk about during the consultation call? Glad you asked. Here's a quick checklist of topics that can be helpful to cover before committing to that first session:

- Your therapy expectations and goals (See Chapter 15)
- The specific circumstance that has inspired you to seek therapy

- If the therapist has any specialization or has worked with others who have been in a similar situation as yourself

- Fees and payment options

- What the cancellation policy is

- Typical length of sessions

- Location of sessions (considering in-person, virtual, or a combination of both)

- Therapist's availability (days and times they have available for scheduling sessions)

- How frequently you'd like to schedule sessions

- The therapist's professional qualifications and experience

- How long the therapist usually works with clients (is it weeks, months, years?)

- Their approach to therapy and what typically happens during sessions

- Next steps for scheduling that first session (if you want to move forward)

Therapists Are Like Good Soles

I once heard a good comparison: finding the right therapist is like finding a great pair of shoes. It might not be the right fit the first time you try a pair on, but we don't let one bad fit discourage us from considering the rest of the shoes out there, right? Some will be the wrong size, another pair might be a little uncomfortable, one might be good for a certain outfit but not everything, the next could be okay enough to keep for a while, but you keep looking until you finally discover your dream pair.

I want you to know that getting discouraged throughout this process is completely normal. It can be tough when you create expectations based on therapist profiles you see online, put in the effort to reach out and schedule consultation calls, only to find yourself starting all over again when it doesn't feel like the right match. I've scrolled through *Psychology Today* myself and envisioned a perfect and natural rapport with a potential therapist, just to speak with someone who turned out to be totally different from the version I had created in my mind. Allow yourself to be surprised by who might end up being a good fit, and remember that sometimes the best therapeutic relationships develop with people you wouldn't have expected. The key is staying open to the process while trusting your instincts about what feels right for you.

Once you've landed on a therapist you'd like to commit to working with, even if it's just to try them out for a few sessions, it's time to start preparing for that crucial first appointment. Remember, this is still part of the evaluation process, so give yourself permission to take your time in deciding whether this will be a good long-term fit.

Chapter 17

What to Expect for Your First Session

So you've searched through the directories, consulted with a therapist, and you're ready to get that first session in the books. Congrats! This is a huge step towards taking care of your mental health. What should you expect before and during your initial appointment? The specifics of the process varies from therapist to therapist, but there are a few general steps that are pretty standard for starting therapy.

Administrative Intake

I totally understand that this part of the process can feel a little impersonal and overwhelming at the start of what may feel like a vulnerable relationship. You might be thinking, "I'm here to talk about my feelings, not fill out forms!" But this administrative groundwork actually helps set the stage for effective therapy.

When it comes to intake, you receive forms to fill out and email back, or you might receive a portal login to be set up in the therapist's electronic file management and payment system. Most therapists try to make this process as streamlined as possible, but there are usually a couple forms or documents that need to be addressed prior to even scheduling the first session that may include:

Payment Information. This includes insurance details if you're using insurance, or credit card information for private pay. If you've established a sliding-scale fee, a reduced-fee, or pro-bono agreement, information on that will likely be outlined here.

Informed Consent. This is a crucial document that outlines your rights as a client and any legal considerations the therapist is obliged to follow. It covers things like confidentiality (what stays between you and your therapist) and its limits, such as mandated reporting situations. These typically include:

- Imminent risk of harm to yourself or others
- Suspicion of child or elder abuse
- Court orders in certain legal situations

Your therapist should review this with you during your first session to ensure you understand when they might need to break confidentiality. This isn't meant to scare you, but rather creates a transparent, ethical relationship from the start.

Clinical and Personal History: This form often includes questions about:

- Previous therapy experiences (what worked, what didn't)
- Current and past medications

- Medical conditions that impact your mental health

- Family mental health history

- Current symptoms you're experiencing

- Major life events or trauma

Even though it can be uncomfortable to write down hard parts of your personal history before you even meet for the first session, this can help your therapist be more helpful when you start working together.

Preparing For the First Session

Talking Points

Walking into your first therapy session can feel overwhelming, and many clients I see regularly even express feeling anxious about not knowing what to talk about. If you'd feel more comfortable walking (or clicking "join") into that first session with talking points, then preparing some thoughts ahead of time can help you make the most of this initial meeting and ensure you address what's most important to you.

EXERCISE 17.1 FIRST SESSION PREP

What brings you to therapy?
Consider what finally prompted you to reach out now. Was there a specific incident, or is it an ongoing struggle? What would you like to be different in your life?

What are your therapy goals?
Like we covered in Chapter 15, what do you want to work on? Even a general idea is helpful.

What are your current barriers?

Reflect on what's currently standing in your way. Consider both external obstacles (work stress, relationship conflicts) and internal barriers (self-doubt, fear, unhelpful thought patterns).

If you had previous therapy experiences, how did they go? If you've worked with therapists before, reflect on what was helpful and what wasn't. This can guide your new therapeutic relationship.

It's Normal to be Nervous

I've heard countless new clients express that they're feeling nervous during their first session. In fact, I have recurring clients whom I see weekly who still feel nervous before sessions, even after working together for months. Nervousness can be fueled by fear of judgment, lack of practice in vulnerability, not feeling ready for change, or anxiety around breaking down in a session. Or worse, according to some of my regular clients, this fear comes from not knowing what to say during that particular session.

All of these fears are understandable, but rest assured that therapists have plenty of practice with helping people to feel comfortable and safe within the therapeutic space. We know that approaching difficult topics might not come easily to all of us. If you find yourself jumping into the deep end of the emotional pool, try to trust that we have the floaties ready at hand to bring you back to safety.

If you find that you're too nervous to have effective interactions in your therapy session, it might be worth addressing that nervousness within the session. As a therapist, I've always found it to be pretty courageous when a client opens up about nervousness within the therapeutic space. It helps me to know when and how I should adjust my approach with that client, and gives me valuable feedback to better understand how that client is thinking and feeling.

If your nerves are in response to sharing space, personal thoughts, and feelings with a professional, remember that therapists are people, too. Therapists often make mistakes and have issues in their own lives. I've joked with my friends and family that being a therapist doesn't make me a perfect person; it does, however, make me cringingly aware of when I'm saying or doing things that might not be the best choice. Therapists often go to therapy themselves! I say all this in hopes of addressing the *white coat syndrome* that people are prone to, which is tension (and typically refers to medically higher blood pressure) around the time of interacting with doctors and people in the medical field.

Remember that your first few meetings with a therapist are as much about you being able to evaluate them as them getting to know you. Sometimes we need a few meetings to fully understand what a working relationship between therapist and client will look like. I often tell clients in the first session that this is your time and your money, so we want it to work for you. Feel free to give feedback and get engaged in the process of therapy so that you can get the most out of it. At the end of the day, you're the one in the driver's seat.

What to Bring With You

Whether you're meeting in-person or in a virtual therapy space, there are a few items that might be useful to have with you during your session. I'd suggest:

A notebook and pen: to write down thoughts you have, questions, ideas, recommendations, or homework.

A water bottle: because talking can be thirsty work! If you're in an office, many times you might even find a tea or hot cocoa station set up for clients.

Questions for the therapist: about their approach or therapeutic style, the therapy process itself, their experience, or even their political beliefs, which is becoming more common in recent years to ask. (See Chapter 16 for more advice.)

A list of topics: if you're worried about forgetting something important.

A comfort item: like a stress ball, or even wearing a favorite body spray. If you're at home, feel free to cuddle up with your favorite blanket or bring in anything else that can help with making you feel grounded.

Payment information: if it's not already on file, this includes your method of payment (a card or checkbook), or your insurance card.

What Actually Happens

A first therapy session usually lasts anywhere between 45 to 60 minutes (with 50 minutes being an industry standard), though it can sometimes extend up to 90 minutes depending on the therapist's preference. You will likely know the amount of time allotted once you receive your appointment confirmation (which usually comes through email, or sometimes via text if you've opted in to text reminders).

Your therapist will likely begin by reviewing the paperwork you've submitted, particularly the informed consent document. They'll explain confidentiality and its limits, their cancellation policy, how to reach them between sessions, and their therapeutic approach. This is your chance to ask any questions about these policies or how therapy works. Don't hesitate to speak up if something is unclear!

At some point after covering the logistics, your therapist will start getting to know you and your history. In my own first sessions, I tell new clients that they're the experts in themselves and I'm just starting from scratch, so any information to get me up to speed is helpful. Your therapist may follow up on information from your intake forms or ask additional questions about your current symptoms or challenges, relevant family or relationship patterns, and what's going right in your life at the moment. This history-taking helps your therapist understand the context of your current struggles and begins to formulate how they might best help you.

Toward the later half of the session, you and your therapist might work towards identifying some preliminary goals for therapy. Remember that the goals may evolve over time (See Chapter 15), but having an initial direction to move in can be helpful.

Before you leave the session, your therapist should give you a sense of what comes next. This could include scheduling the next session and discussing frequency of appointments, or their initial evaluation of what's going on in your life and what might be helpful. If you select a therapist who uses "homework" between sessions, they're likely to explain what the exercises entail either at the end of the session or via email if appropriate.

And just like that, you've made it through the first session! I recommend taking some time to process on your own once it ends. Take note of what you liked and which parts of the session may not sit right with you. Walking or driving back home from in-person sessions can be a great buffer time to readjust back into reality. If you joined a virtual session, you may need to be more intentional in taking time and space to reflect and immerse back into the rest of your daily routine.

A Critical Next Step in Your Mental Health Journey
Taking that first step into therapy is courageous. By preparing thoughtfully for your initial session, you're already actively participating in your mental health journey. Finding the right therapeutic relationship can sometimes take time, but when it clicks, it can be one of the most valuable relationships in your life.

Chapter 18

Making the Most of Therapy

Therapy is an active journey, not a passive experience. It's not uncommon for someone new to therapy to enter their first session expecting the therapist to "fix" them, only to discover that the key to long-lasting change happens through putting in the work themselves. The therapeutic hour represents just a fraction of your week—what you do with the rest of your time outside of the therapeutic space often determines the progress towards your therapeutic goals. This chapter explores how to maximize every aspect of your therapy experience, from preparation and engagement during sessions to practice between appointments and eventually transitioning out of therapy.

Like any worthwhile endeavor, therapy requires investment; not just financial, but emotional and practical. Putting in time and energy to your growth and healing can accelerate the process of improving your mental health and well-being. If this sounds overwhelming, the good news is that there are concrete steps you can take to become an active participant in your healing journey, accelerate your progress, and develop skills that will serve you long after therapy concludes.

Optimizing Your Therapy Sessions

Preparing for Productive Sessions

Unless you've determined that you want to explore your subconscious and practice free association, walking into therapy without preparation can feel like showing up to an important meeting without an agenda. You are likely to cover something useful, but you might miss crucial topics if you're not being intentional. Effective preparation doesn't need to be time-consuming, however; even 5 minutes of reflection before your session can dramatically increase its value.

Consider keeping a simple note in your phone or journal where you jot down moments throughout the week when you think, "I should bring this up in therapy." (If you're anything like me, you might be thinking that you'll remember that thought when the session arrives just to experience your mind blanking out when it's go time.) Take time before your session to review these notes. You might choose one or two priorities you want to address in the session, or you might surprise yourself and find that they're no longer concerns.

Creating a transitional block of time before therapy can help your mind shift from being caught up in daily life to a more reflective, introspective state. For virtual sessions, I'd suggest finding a private space where you won't be interrupted and allow yourself at least a couple minutes of quiet before joining the session. Putting your phone on mute or airplane mode would also be helpful in making sure you'll be focused throughout your session.

For in-person appointments, see if you can arrive early enough to sit in your car or a waiting area to collect your thoughts. Joining your session in a rush, whether virtual or in-person, can have you feeling scrambled and gets in the way of being grounded. Buffer time allows you to arrive mentally, along with physically, and thus makes it easier to engage in meaningful work once your session begins.

Finally, approaching therapy with an open mind and with intentionality will take you far in your therapy journey. Meaningful growth often emerges when we're able to allow ourselves to feel vulnerable or uncertain, which can be an uncomfortable practice for many of us. Think about your mind like a muscle doing weight training—the resistance causes some discomfort in the moment but leads to strength and resilience.

If you ever catch yourself thinking, "I don't want to talk about that" or "This feels too uncomfortable," try to lean in instead of disengaging if it's safe for you to do so. Equally important is viewing your therapist as a skilled collaborator in your healing journey instead of an authority figure with all the answers. Even though they may bring knowledge in the field of psychology, you're still the expert on your own experience. The most productive therapeutic relationships balance your therapist's professional knowledge with your personal insight, creating a partnership where both perspectives are valued and neither person holds all the power.

Engaging Fully During Sessions

Practicing honest communication can make a world of difference when it comes to deeply engaging in therapy. This is more for your benefit than for the therapist's sake. While the instinct to appear "put together" is understandable, it ultimately slows your progress.

Including the messy, uncomfortable parts of yourself in session that you might prefer to hide helps you acknowledge and accept your whole reality. Your therapist isn't there to judge you but to understand your authentic experience, and you might find that having your therapist accept the shadier parts of your past or present can be healing in itself. When you're in therapy, or even with trusted loved ones, practice noticing when you're filtering your thoughts and gently challenge yourself to share one thing you might normally hold back.

On the topic of *mindfulness* (see Chapter 12), you might find this to be transformative both in and out of therapy. Mentally rehearsing what you'll say in therapy is not uncommon, as well as talking while on autopilot or keeping the conversation surface-level to avoid deeper processing. But instead of going down these avenues, try approaching each session with intentional curiosity about what's going on in your mind and body from moment to moment.

When your therapist asks how you're feeling, pause to check in with your body before responding. What sensations are you experiencing? Is there tightness in your chest, warmth in your face, or a sinking feeling in your stomach? These physical cues often reveal emotions that your conscious mind hasn't yet acknowledged. Being able to stay present with bodily sensations and difficult emotions, rather than intellectualizing or distracting from them, is one of the hardest skills to learn. It's also one of the most foundational skills in therapy. Once you're able to master this in therapy, you'll become unstoppable at understanding and regulating emotions out in the real world.

But if you're having a hard time staying in the present moment during your session, you can ask your therapist for help. My own therapist is fantastic at having me check in with my body when she senses that I'm skipping this tune-in. Don't hesitate to ask your therapist for a pause or to let them know if you're feeling lost or overwhelmed. Sometimes a simple "I don't understand, can you explain?" or "I'm feeling a bit overwhelmed—can we take a moment?" creates space for deeper understanding and more authentic engagement in session.

The therapeutic relationship itself also provides valuable information about how you relate to others. Pay attention to moments when you feel particularly connected to your therapist, as well as times when you feel misunderstood or resistant. These patterns often mirror dynamics in your outside relationships. Instead of keeping these thoughts and feelings to yourself, consider bringing them into the conversation. Saying, "I'm feeling defensive right now," or "Wow, that observation really resonated with me," can deepen the therapeutic impact and build your communication skills for all relationships.

I've had clients even say "Hey, I got pretty mad at you the last time we met," which has been fantastic for clarifying misunderstandings and learning about how my clients process different types of interpersonal interactions. It's also easy to assume that therapists will be offended by constructive criticism or that expressing preferences means you may be labeled a difficult client. In reality, most therapists welcome your input on what's working and what isn't. If a particular exercise feels especially helpful, say so! If an approach isn't resonating or you're confused about the purpose of an intervention, speak up.

This kind of feedback helps your therapist tailor treatment to your unique needs and learning style. Although this might not be the popular opinion of therapists, my belief is that therapy is ultimately a service you're investing in. In this economy (or any economy), neither you nor your therapist benefits from continuing with approaches that don't contribute to the improvement of your mental health. Good therapy evolves based on your experience and feedback, and being comfortable in therapy helps with engaging and growing.

Practicing Between Sessions

The real magic and impact of therapy is not always what happens in sessions. You're likely to find that more improvement happens when you're applying the new insights and tools from appointments to your everyday life. If you were roped into playing a musical instrument as a kid, you'll remember that the more you practiced at home, the better you were able to perform at school. But if you were like me and didn't feel like busting out the cello on your days off, then you might have been seated far away from the first chair like yours truly.

Weekly sessions can provide life-changing feedback and understanding, but only when you carry those lessons into your routine are you able to achieve mastery. Without regular practice, you'll miss out on feeling and living the change. (And that last part is what makes a long-lasting impact!) As I've said before and I'll say again (and again and again), start small and work your way up with the changes. Consistency and dedication to a small adjustment is much more approachable and sustainable than starting off with fifty small changes or a single enormous one.

Remember that your brain gets *physically altered* through repeated practice, which gives your neurons the chance to form and strengthen new pathways. Setting boundaries, practicing self-compassion, or challenging negative thoughts will likely feel awkward or forced at first. But with repetition, it becomes more natural.

If you find that it's tough to consistently practice what you've learned in therapy, approach the struggle with curiosity. I find that clients are often embarrassed if they haven't practiced the skill we had talked about, or they make some self-critical remarks. I remind them that not practicing the skills or concepts can be useful feedback. If you're experiencing some resistance to "walking the walk" after "talking the talk," bring it up to your therapist. There might be an underlying belief or assumption blocking the way, or your application of the skill might need to be tweaked to be easier to implement in your specific circumstances. If you're able to avoid that inner critic and feelings of discouragement, you'll likely find that you're able to get better at practicing between sessions. Hey, you might even experience some breakthroughs in treatment.

Navigating Challenges in Therapy

Addressing Discomfort and Resistance

The struggle we just touched on with actually doing therapeutic homework isn't the only place where resistance can pop up. As we already touched on, you might also notice it *during* the therapy session. Experiencing discomfort in therapy doesn't necessarily signal that something is wrong. Barring ethical and moral dilemmas in therapy, discomfort and resistance can often indicate that you're doing something right. Growth requires pushing past your comfort zone and venturing into territory that can feel vulnerable or uncertain.

If you're starting to feel uncomfortable in therapy, investigate the feeling and try to see if it is either *productive discomfort* or *unproductive distress* (See Chapter 11). Productive discomfort is the temporary unease that comes with growth. (Emphasis on temporary!) You might feel productive discomfort when digging into a painful memory or engaging in a tough conversation that you've been avoiding. Even though these experiences are challenging, they move the needle in the right direction and lead you to new insights and relief once you've worked through them.

Unproductive distress, on the other hand, is more harmful than helpful. This could look like feeling unsafe physically or emotionally while working with your therapist, or running into a misunderstanding that isn't getting resolved and therefore hinders progress in therapy. If your gut is telling you that something you're experiencing in therapy is wrong, seek feedback from people you trust and move forward in a way that best protects your physical and emotional safety. Your therapist should never threaten you, pressure or manipulate you, try to create a personal relationship with you outside of therapy, engage in sexual or romantic relationships with clients, or intentionally violate your boundaries. While it's luckily a small percentage of therapists in this pool, keep in mind that therapy is meant to be a safe place for you. If discomfort is moving from manageable to unsafe, take the precautions that are in your best interest and report anything dangerous or unethical to the local state licensing board.

A final and sneaky phase of therapy to be on the lookout for is hitting a plateau in therapy. When I think about these plateaus, I always picture the P90X commercials that plagued cable TV in the early 2000s—they emphasized that when your progress seems to stall, it's time to kick your activity up a notch. I have to admit that this approach applies well to therapy.

When you reach a plateau in therapy, it's tempting to conclude you've gotten all you can from the process. And sometimes that really is the case: treatment goals have been reached, life has been breezy lately, and it's time to graduate. Other times, there may be some hidden resistance that is keeping you from peeling back the layers of your emotions and experiences. During these periods, collaboration with your therapist can be especially important.

Together, you might need to adjust your approach, dive deeper into topics you've previously scratched the surface of, or identify subtle thoughts or beliefs that are keeping you stuck. Sometimes the plateau itself reveals important information about your patterns, like your habits of avoidance or being selective in processing emotions. But again, bringing up a plateau with your therapist, if they don't bring it up first, can help determine the right path forward.

Managing the Therapeutic Relationship

You might find that even if you do the extensive online search for a therapist, you like how the consultation went, but after some time working together, you're not so sure that they're the right fit for you. This can happen, and that's okay! Don't be afraid to tell your therapist that things aren't working out. Although admittedly this can be a scary conversation to have, it's also a great opportunity to practice communication skills while advocating for yourself.

When any of my clients have told me "Hey, I think I want a different therapist," my first reaction is always amazement and pride that they are able to broach such a difficult topic in session. Is that hard to believe? I know there can be fear of upsetting your therapist or nervousness that they might try to talk you into staying, but the truth is that being able to advocate for your needs to achieve improved mental health is the ultimate goal of therapy. If expressing that you think another therapist might get you there helps you achieve that goal, then I am more than thrilled for you.

There are also instances where the therapist realizes that the client might benefit from working with another professional. I've chatted with colleagues in case discussions where we notice that a client may see more improvement through a Dialectical Behavior Therapy approach but our strength is in narrative processing, for example. In these instances, the therapist may recommend referring you to a differently specialized professional or they may work with you until you're ready to switch up therapy. (See Chapter 16 on Finding the Right Therapist.)

No matter what, your therapist wants the best for you. If you just can't get the energy to do the exercises between sessions, or you feel hesitant in certain session conversations, you'll be better supported in the long run if you bring these feelings up to your therapist. Having this conversation doesn't mean either of you has failed. In fact, it actually demonstrates your commitment to your mental health and efforts of self-advocacy. A professional therapist will respond to these concerns constructively, by either adapting their approach or helping you transition to someone who might be a better fit.

Maintaining Progress and Beyond

Developing Independence

As you get into a flow with your therapist and you progress through the therapeutic process, you'll find that you start to internalize the skills and perspectives that previously were only accessed during the sessions. If you've ever seen the *Inside Out* movies, you may be familiar with the idea of different emotions trying to control the switchboard in your mind. Imagine that the voice of your therapist or the embodiment of your therapeutic lessons now also become one of the characters present at that switchboard. This internalization helps shift your thoughts, feelings, and behavior once it has a presence.

Luckily, this internalization process happens naturally as you practice therapeutic techniques and achieve more independence from your therapist over time. Creating a formal maintenance plan takes this a step further and makes the internalization transition more intentional. As you start to recognize that you may be ready to wind down in therapy and continue moving forward in life on your own, it is helpful to start working with your therapist on creating a post-therapy plan.

The best plans for life outside of regular therapy will incorporate strategies that have been most helpful during the process, potential future challenges that might arise, and concrete plans for managing them. Ideally, you'll also throw in some self-care plans as well. What practices will help you feel your best when things are going well, and which ones will lift you up or at least keep you going when times get tough? Identify the practices that reliably help you feel grounded and regulated, whether that's movement, creative expression, time in nature, or connected moments with loved ones. Schedule these activities with the same commitment you've shown to therapy appointments, recognizing that maintaining your mental health requires ongoing attention and care.

This plan becomes your personalized roadmap for continuing growth beyond the formal therapeutic relationship. Having your plan documented can be, sometimes literally, a lifesaver when things get rocky in the future. We tend to forget our roadmap if it was made a few years ago, so being able to dig it up and remember the key points from the last time you had to navigate your way to well-being can be handy. Consider even keeping your plan somewhere quickly accessible, like your Notes app, email, or cloud drive.

Ending Therapy Successfully

There's a surprising link between dating apps and therapy that I joke about with clients every once in a while. For a little context, the dating app Hinge had a really catchy marketing phrase that continues to stick in my brain: "designed to be deleted." Those four simple words get to the heart of why dating apps exist. In an ideal scenario, we download the app, match with the love of our life, and delete the app for good as we sail off into the sunset.

I think the best-case outcome for therapy is much the same. We find a great therapist to work with, experience healing and gather tools to succeed in the future, and wave goodbye to the therapist as we confidently go forth to conquer the rest of what life has to offer. To boil down the rose-colored-glasses ideal, the whole point of going to therapy is to be able to stop going to therapy.

The decision to end therapy often emerges gradually as you notice greater confidence in handling challenges, decreased distress in previously triggering situations, and an overall sense that you've been able to implement therapeutic strategies on your own. We want to avoid feeling overly dependent on therapists because, at the end of the day, having confidence in your own ability to handle life's ups and downs will give you the best outcome when you reach those polarizing experiences.

Even if therapy has been an amazing experience for you, floating the idea of ending sessions to your therapist can still be intimidating. You might be worried of giving off the impression that you're rejecting your therapist as they're no longer needed, or feel uncomfortable about ending a relationship, including a professional and therapeutic one. I invite you to reframe this termination conversation as a milestone to be celebrated. You've put in the work, reaped the benefits, and now it's time to "graduate" to your next phase.

That said, moving on from therapy is usually more of a transition process than an abrupt ending. Once you broach the topic of ending sessions with your therapist, they are likely to recommend tapering sessions before coming to a full stop. If you're booking appointments weekly, you'll likely move to every other week, then monthly to practice independence while keeping professional connection and support during the transition. I've even heard of some therapists who offer an annual "checkup" therapy session for continued support.

As you work your way to that final session, take time for some reflection and celebration. After all, you've invested significant time, energy, and resources in your growth. During your final sessions, work with your therapist to acknowledge the progress you've made, reviewing where you started and how far you've come. Don't be shy about feeling proud of yourself! You may not have miraculously solved all of life's challenges, but by this point, you've developed the tools to navigate them with greater skill and self-compassion.

Applying the Insights You've Developed

The therapeutic journey doesn't end when formal therapy concludes. In many ways, that's when the most important work begins. Spending months learning to drive with an instructor only to then say, "Great, I've graduated! Now I'll never drive again" sounds a bit silly, right? The same applies to therapy. You get to totally own the insights and skills you've developed as you continue applying them independently, thereby taking the wheel of your own mental health journey.

Many people engage in therapy at different points throughout their lives, returning during particularly challenging moments or when they're ready to work on new aspects of their growth. This isn't regression, but a sign of self-awareness and commitment to your well-being. Each time you return, you're building on the foundation you've already established. Also, if you return to the same therapist, they might even be secretly pleased to see you again!

Ultimately, successful therapy transforms your relationship with yourself. The compassionate, curious perspective from therapy gradually becomes your own internal voice. That critical inner roommate who used to berate you for every minor mistake ("You forgot to buy milk *again*? You absolute disaster of a human!") gets replaced by a more understanding presence. You become better at recognizing your patterns, understanding your needs, and responding to your struggles with kindness rather than criticism. These changes ripple outward, affecting your relationships, work, and approach to life's inevitable challenges.

While therapy itself may be temporary, its impact can last a lifetime. The goal isn't to become someone who never struggles (oh, how I wish that was possible!), but rather someone who knows how to navigate those struggles with greater wisdom and a more advanced skillset. You'll still have moments when you slip into old patterns, but you'll catch yourself faster and recover more effectively. Eventually, you might even find yourself saying things to friends that sound suspiciously like something your therapist would say. (At which point, you can either send them a royalty check or simply appreciate how thoroughly you've integrated their wisdom.) Either way, you'll know the investment you made in therapy continues paying dividends long after your final session.

Acknowledgements

As a Muslim, I first and foremost have to thank my Creator for planting the idea for this book in my head. I remember asking fellow author, Bonita Hampton Smith, about how she came up with the idea for her book *Dear White Woman, Dear Black Woman*. She replied "It was like a download," and I can think of no better description for how the inspiration for *I Didn't Want to Either* entered my mind.

Being able to write this book during countless nights and my baby's nap times (which were all too short), while living abroad, working California hours, and managing a full family life felt like a divine intervention. Looking back, I'm still puzzled as to how this book came together because it certainly couldn't have been solely from my own efforts.

For the fellow humans who helped this project come together, I have to thank my husband who waited patiently as I delayed date nights and TV binges for the sake of word counts and chapter outlining. Your support made this work possible, even when it meant explaining to family that I was once again "having a moment with my laptop." And a quick note of appreciation to the family cat, Harry, for keeping me and my laptop company even if it included some kitty snoring.

To the incredible professors at the University of San Francisco's Master's in Counseling Psychology program, particularly Dr. Belinda Hernandez-Arriaga—thank you for seeing something in my application that warranted acceptance into the program, and for teaching me the foundations of everything I know about being a therapist. Your wisdom echoes through these pages.

My deepest gratitude to my clinical supervisors who graciously opened their therapeutic lenses and let me peek inside: Lettie Villavicencio, Ari-Asha Castalia, Simi Markar, and especially Rana Chawla, whose brain I am determined to continue picking for the rest of my career. You each shaped not just my clinical approach but the therapist (and human) I've become.

I'm deeply grateful to my clients, who were a source of motivation for creating a resource such as this book. Every session has taught me something new about resilience, courage, and the human capacity for growth. While I may have provided the therapeutic framework, you've done the hard work, and I've learned immensely from watching you navigate your journeys. Thank you for trusting me with your stories.

To the phenomenal team at Ripples Media—this book would have died a quiet death in my notes app alongside my many other passionate-but-unfinished projects if not for you. Andrew Vogel, thank you for the guidance and accountability that transformed scattered ideas into actual chapters. Nicole Wedekind, your clear insight kept me on track. DMF, your tight and clean timelines brought us home in the end. And Burtch Hunter, thank you for the beautiful design work, especially while your personal life sounded as chaotic as mine during this project.

A special thank you to my editor Terra Elan McVoy, who deserves her own paragraph. (Or perhaps her own chapter.) Terra cheered me on when I needed encouragement, taught me about the writing process when I was scratching my head, and gently told me when things I wrote had, well, sucked and needed improvement. She has become my role model for what a writer should be, and I'm half-debating writing another book just for the pleasure of working with her again. Thank you, Terra, for making me a better writer and for believing in this project with me.

And finally, to you, the reader: I wrote this entire book for you. I support you from afar in your journey toward better mental health, and I hope these pages provide some guidance, comfort, or insight when you need it most. Thank you for picking up this book and for having the courage to invest in yourself.

Bibliography

Abdaal, Ali. *Feel-Good Productivity: How to Do More of What Matters to You*. New York, NY: Celadon Books, 2023.

Agathos, James, Trevor Steward, Christopher G. Davey, Kim L. Felmingham, Sevil Ince, Bradford A. Moffat, Rebecca K. Glarin, and Ben J. Harrison. "Differential engagement of the posterior cingulate cortex during cognitive restructuring of negative self-and social beliefs." Social cognitive and affective neuroscience 18, no. 1 (2023): nsad024.

Attia, Peter, and Bill Gifford. *Outlive: The Science & Art of Longevity*. New York, NY: Harmony, 2023.

Borhade MB, Yashi K, Singh S. Diabetes and Exercise. [Updated 2025 Feb 26]. In: StatPearls [Internet]. Treasure Island (FL): StatPearls Publishing; 2025 Jan-. Available from: https://www.ncbi.nlm.nih.gov/books/NBK526095/

Bornstein, Marc H., and Gianluca Esposito. "Coregulation: A multilevel approach via biology and behavior." Children 10, no. 8 (2023): 1323.

Bronfenbrenner, U. *Six Theories of Child Development: Revised Formulations and Current Issues*. Edited by R. Vasta, Jessica Kingsley Publishers, 1992, pp. 187–249.

Cameron, Julia. *The Artist's Way: A Spiritual Path to Higher Creativity*. London, UK: Macmillan, 2016.

Chapman, Gary D. *The 5 Love Languages: The Secret to Love That Lasts*. Chicago, IL: Northfield Publishing, 2015.

Chu, Brianna, Komal Marwaha, Terrence Sanvictores, Ayoola O. Awosika, and Derek Ayers. "Physiology, stress reaction." In StatPearls [Internet]. StatPearls Publishing, 2024.

Ciarrochi, Joseph, Steven C. Hayes, Lindsay G. Oades, and Stefan G. Hofmann. "Toward a unified framework for positive psychology interventions: Evidence-based processes of change in coaching, prevention, and training." Frontiers in psychology 12 (2022): 809362.

Cohen, Sheldon, and Thomas A. Wills. "Stress, social support, and the buffering hypothesis." Psychological bulletin 98, no. 2 (1985): 310.

Connor-Greene, P. A. (2000). Making Connections: Evaluating the Effectiveness of Journal Writing in Enhancing Student Learning. Teaching of Psychology, 27(1), 44-46. https://doi.org/10.1207/S15328023TOP2701_10 (APA FORMAT!)

Darwall-Smith, Heather. *The Science of Sleep: Stop Chasing a Good Night's Sleep and Let It Find You*. London, UK: DK, 2021.

Duhigg, Charles. *The Power of Habit: Why We Do What We Do in Life and Business*. New York, NY: Random House Trade Paperbacks, 2012.

Evans-Martin, Fay. *The Human Body (The Nervous System: How It Works)*. 3rd ed. New York, NY: Chelsea House, 2010.

Frankl, Viktor E. *Man's Search for Meaning*. Boston, MA: Beacon Press, 2006.

Gold, Katherine J., Margaret L. Dobson, and Ananda Sen. ""Three good things" digital intervention among health care workers: a randomized controlled trial." The Annals of Family Medicine 21, no. 3 (2023): 220-226.

Hegberg, Nicole J., Jasmeet P. Hayes, and Scott M. Hayes. "Exercise intervention in PTSD: A narrative review and rationale for implementation." Frontiers in psychiatry 10 (2019): 133.

Ignácio, Zuleide M et al. "Physical Exercise and Neuroinflammation in Major Depressive Disorder." Molecular neurobiology vol. 56,12 (2019): 8323-8335. doi:10.1007/s12035-019-01670-1

Juvonen, Jaana, Leah M. Lessard, Naomi G. Kline, and Sandra Graham. "Young adult adaptability to the social challenges of the COVID-19 pandemic: The protective role of friendships." Journal of Youth and Adolescence 51, no. 3 (2022): 585-597.

Kandola, A., Stubbs, B. (2020). Exercise and Anxiety. In: Xiao, J. (eds) Physical Exercise for Human Health. Advances in Experimental Medicine and Biology, vol 1228. Springer, Singapore. https://doi.org/10.1007/978-981-15-1792-1_23

Kirsten Hötting, Brigitte Röder, Beneficial effects of physical exercise on neuroplasticity and cognition, Neuroscience & Biobehavioral Reviews, Volume 37, Issue 9, Part B, 2013, Pages 2243-2257, ISSN 0149-7634, https://doi.org/10.1016/j.neubiorev.2013.04.005.

Lafer, Beny, Cicera Claudinea Duarte, Julia Maria D'Andrea Greve, Paulo Roberto dos Santos Silva, Karla Mathias de Almeida, Gabriel Okawa Belizario, and Lucas Melo Neves. "Structured physical exercise for bipolar depression: an open-label, proof-of concept study." International journal of bipolar disorders 11, no. 1 (2023): 14.

Linehan, Marsha. *Cognitive-Behavioral Treatment for Borderline Personality Disorder*. New York, NY: The Guilford Press, 1993.

Liu Y, Wheaton AG, Chapman DP, Cunningham TJ, Lu H, Croft JB. Prevalence of Healthy Sleep Duration among Adults—United States, 2014. MMWR Morb Mortal Wkly Rep 2016;65:137–141.

Marano, Giuseppe, Georgios D. Kotzalidis, Francesco Maria Lisci, Maria Benedetta Anesini, Sara Rossi, Sara Barbonetti, Andrea Cangini et al. "The Neuroscience Behind Writing: Handwriting vs. Typing—Who Wins the Battle?." Life 15, no. 3 (2025): 345.

Maté, Gabor. *When the Body Says No: Understanding the Stress-disease Connection*. Hoboken, NJ: J. Wiley, 2003.

Naidoo, Uma. *This Is Your Brain on Food: An Indispensable Guide to the Surprising Foods that Fight Depression, Anxiety, PTSD, OCD, ADHD, and More*. New York, NY: Little, Brown Spark, 2020.

Naidoo, Uma. *Calm Your Mind with Food: A Revolutionary Guide to Controlling Your Anxiety*. New York, NY: Little, Brown Spark, 2023.

Nakao, Mutsuhiro, Kentaro Shirotsuki, and Nagisa Sugaya. "Cognitive–behavioral therapy for management of mental health and stress-related disorders: Recent advances in techniques and technologies." BioPsychoSocial medicine 15, no. 1 (2021): 16.

National Sleep Foundation, blog post https://www.thensf.org/how-many-hours-of-sleep-do-you-really-need/

Newman, David B., Amie M. Gordon, and Wendy Berry Mendes. "Comparing daily physiological and psychological benefits of gratitude and optimism using a digital platform." Emotion 21, no. 7 (2021): 1357.

Prochaska, J. O., and C. C. Diclemente. 'Stages and Processes of Self-Change of Smoking: Toward an Integrative Model of Change'. Journal of Consulting and Clinical Psychology, vol. 51, no. 3, 1983, pp. 390–395.

Ratey, John J., and Eric Hagerman. *Spark: The Revolutionary New Science of Exercise and the Brain.* New York, NY: Little, Brown Spark, 2013.

Shen B, Ma C, Wu G, Liu H, Chen L, Yang G. Effects of exercise on circadian rhythms in humans. Front Pharmacol. 2023 Oct 11;14:1282357. doi: 10.3389/fphar.2023.1282357. PMID: 37886134; PMCID: PMC10598774.

Seligman, Martin. *Flourish: A Visionary New Understanding of Happiness and Well-being.* New York, NY: Simon Acumen, 2012.

Smith, Patrick J., and Rhonda M. Merwin. "The role of exercise in management of mental health disorders: an integrative review." Annual review of medicine 72, no. 1 (2021): 45-62.

Stanton, Robert, and Peter Reaburn. "Exercise and the treatment of depression: a review of the exercise program variables." Journal of science and medicine in sport 17, no. 2 (2014): 177-182.

Steindl-Rast, David (2013) TEDGlobal ted talk video

Walker, Matthew, 2019 ted talk

Willcox, Gloria. "The Feeling Wheel: A Tool for Expanding Awareness of Emotions and Increasing Spontaneity and Intimacy." Transactional Analysis Journal, vol. 12, no. 3, 1982, pp. 274–276.

Vysniauske, Ruta, Lot Verburgh, Jaap Oosterlaan, and Marc L. Molendijk. "The effects of physical exercise on functional outcomes in the treatment of ADHD: a meta-analysis." Journal of attention disorders 24, no. 5 (2020): 644-654.

Zaboski, Romaker, and Diana Joyce-Beauclieu. "Theory and Research." In *Applied Cognitive Behavioral Therapy in Schools*, edited
by Diana Joyce-Beaulieu and Brian A. Zaboski, 25-45. New York, NY:
Oxford University Press, 2021.

Struthless (2024) https://www.youtube.com/watch?v=U8RQsJ0Q3Mo

www.ingramcontent.com/pod-product-compliance
Lightning Source LLC
Chambersburg PA
CBHW021218130626
46554CB00004B/1271